California
HMH SCIENCE DIMENSIONS™
Volume 3

Grade 7
Units 6–7

Watch the cover come alive as you adjust factors for plant growth.
Download the HMH Science Dimensions AR app available on Android or iOS devices.

This Write-In Book belongs to

Vladimir Rivera

Teacher/Room

Houghton Mifflin Harcourt™

Consulting Authors

Michael A. DiSpezio

Global Educator
North Falmouth,
Massachusetts

Michael DiSpezio has authored many HMH instructional programs for Science and Mathematics. He has also authored numerous trade books and multimedia programs on various topics and hosted dozens of studio and location broadcasts for various organizations in the United States and worldwide. Most recently, he has been working with educators to provide strategies for implementing the Next Generation Science Standards, particularly the Science and Engineering Practices, Crosscutting Concepts, and the use of Evidence Notebooks. To all his projects, he brings his extensive background in science, his expertise in classroom teaching at the elementary, middle, and high school levels, and his deep experience in producing interactive and engaging instructional materials.

Marjorie Frank

Science Writer and Content-Area Reading Specialist
Brooklyn, New York

An educator and linguist by training, a writer and poet by nature, Marjorie Frank has authored and designed a generation of instructional materials in all subject areas, including past HMH Science programs. Her other credits include authoring science issues of an award-winning children's magazine, writing game-based digital assessments, developing blended learning materials for young children, and serving as instructional designer and coauthor of pioneering school-to-work software. In addition, she has served on the adjunct faculty of Hunter, Manhattan, and Brooklyn Colleges, teaching courses in science methods, literacy, and writing. For *California HMH Science Dimensions™*, she has guided the development of our K–2 strands and our approach to making connections between NGSS and Common Core ELA/literacy standards.

Acknowledgments

Cover credits: (plant) ©HMH; (Earth at night) ©Nastco/iStock/Getty Images Plus/Getty Images.

Section Header Master Art: (machinations) ©DNY59/E+/Getty Images; (rivers on top of Greenland ice sheet) ©Maria-José Viñas, NASA Earth Science News Team; (human cells, illustration) ©Sebastian Kaulitzki/Science Photo Library/Corbis; (waves) ©Alfred Pasieka/Science Source

Printed in the U.S.A.

ISBN 978-0-358-22122-7

3 4 5 6 7 8 9 10 0877 27 26 25 24 23 22 21

4500817312   B C D E F G

Michael R. Heithaus, PhD

Dean, College of Arts, Sciences & Education Professor, Department of Biological Sciences
Florida International University
Miami, Florida

Mike Heithaus joined the FIU Biology Department in 2003 and has served as Director of the Marine Sciences Program and Executive Director of the School of Environment, Arts, and Society, which brings together the natural and social sciences and humanities to develop solutions to today's environmental challenges. He now serves as Dean of the College of Arts, Sciences & Education. His research focuses on predator-prey interactions and the ecological importance of large marine species. He has helped to guide the development of Life Science content in *California HMH Science Dimensions*™, with a focus on strategies for teaching challenging content as well as the science and engineering practices of analyzing data and using computational thinking.

Bernadine Okoro

Access and Equity Consultant

S.T.E.M. Learning Advocate & Consultant
Washington, DC

Bernadine Okoro is a chemical engineer by training and a playwright, novelist, director, and actress by nature. Okoro went from working with patents and biotechnology to teaching in K–12 classrooms. A 12-year science educator and Albert Einstein Distinguished Fellow, Okoro was one of the original authors of the Next Generation Science Standards. As a member of the Diversity and Equity Team, her focus on Alternative Education and Community Schools and on Integrating Social-Emotional Learning and Brain-Based Learning into NGSS is the vehicle she uses as a pathway to support underserved groups from elementary school to adult education. An article and book reviewer for NSTA and other educational publishing companies, Okoro currently works as a S.T.E.M. Learning Advocate & Consultant.

Cary I. Sneider, PhD

Associate Research Professor
Portland State University
Portland, Oregon

While studying astrophysics at Harvard, Cary Sneider volunteered to teach in an Upward Bound program and discovered his real calling as a science teacher. After teaching middle and high school science in Maine, California, Costa Rica, and Micronesia, he settled for nearly three decades at Lawrence Hall of Science in Berkeley, California, where he developed skills in curriculum development and teacher education. Over his career, Cary directed more than 20 federal, state, and foundation grant projects and was a writing team leader for the Next Generation Science Standards. He has been instrumental in ensuring *California HMH Science Dimensions*™ meets the high expectations of the NGSS and provides an effective three-dimensional learning experience for all students.

Program Advisors

Paul D. Asimow, PhD
Eleanor and John R. McMillan
Professor of Geology and
Geochemistry
California Institute of Technology
Pasadena, California

Joanne Bourgeois
Professor Emerita
Earth & Space Sciences
University of Washington
Seattle, WA

Dr. Eileen Cashman
Professor
Humboldt State University
Arcata, California

Elizabeth A. De Stasio, PhD
Raymond J. Herzog Professor of
Science
Lawrence University
Appleton, Wisconsin

Perry Donham, PhD
Lecturer
Boston University
Boston, Massachusetts

Shila Garg, PhD
Professor Emerita of Physics
Former Dean of Faculty & Provost
The College of Wooster
Wooster, Ohio

Tatiana A. Krivosheev, PhD
Professor of Physics
Clayton State University
Morrow, Georgia

Mark B. Moldwin, PhD
Professor of Space Sciences and
Engineering
University of Michigan
Ann Arbor, Michigan

Ross H. Nehm
Stony Brook University (SUNY)
Stony Brook, NY

Kelly Y. Neiles, PhD
Assistant Professor of Chemistry
St. Mary's College of Maryland
St. Mary's City, Maryland

John Nielsen-Gammon, PhD
Regents Professor
Department of Atmospheric
Sciences
Texas A&M University
College Station, Texas

Dr. Sten Odenwald
Astronomer
NASA Goddard Spaceflight Center
Greenbelt, Maryland

Bruce W. Schafer
Executive Director
Oregon Robotics Tournament &
Outreach Program
Beaverton, Oregon

Barry A. Van Deman
President and CEO
Museum of Life and Science
Durham, North Carolina

Kim Withers, PhD
Assistant Professor
Texas A&M University-Corpus
Christi
Corpus Christi, Texas

Adam D. Woods, PhD
Professor
California State University,
Fullerton
Fullerton, California

English Development Advisors

Mercy D. Momary
Local District Northwest
Los Angeles, California

Michelle Sullivan
Balboa Elementary
San Diego, California

Lab Safety Reviewer

Kenneth R. Roy, Ph.D.
Senior Lab Safety Compliance Consultant
National Safety Consultants, LLC
Vernon, Connecticut

Classroom Reviewers & Hands-On Activities Advisors

Julie Arreola
Sun Valley Magnet School
Sun Valley, California

Pamela Bluestein
Sycamore Canyon School
Newbury Park, California

Andrea Brown
HLPUSD Science & STEAM TOSA
Hacienda Heights, California

Stephanie Greene
Science Department Chair
Sun Valley Magnet School
Sun Valley, California

Rana Mujtaba Khan
Will Rogers High School
Van Nuys, California

Suzanne Kirkhope
Willow Elementary and Round
Meadow Elementary
Agoura Hills, California

George Kwong
Schafer Park Elementary
Hayward, California

Imelda Madrid
Bassett St. Elementary School
Lake Balboa, California

Susana Martinez O'Brien
Diocese of San Diego
San Diego, California

Craig Moss
Mt. Gleason Middle School
Sunland, California

Isabel Souto
Schafer Park Elementary
Hayward, California

Emily R.C.G. Williams
South Pasadena Middle School
South Pasadena, California

© Houghton Mifflin Harcourt Publishing Company • Image Credits: (t) ©Gabriel Bouys/
AFP/Getty Images; (b) ©G. Brad Lewis/Aurora/Getty Images

VOLUME 1

UNIT 3 Chemical Processes

133

This is a crystal of progesterone, an important hormone in the human body. It can be synthetically produced from plant materials using a series of chemical reactions known as the Marker Degradation.

VOLUME 2

UNIT 4 Matter and Energy in Organisms and Rock 225

Mountain goats feed and play on the rocky peaks formed by Earth's processes.

VOLUME 2

UNIT 5 Earth's Resources and Ecosystems

315

We depend on forests for many resources, including paper, furniture, medicines, and biofuels.

CONTENTS IN THIS VOLUME

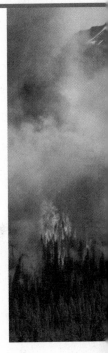
© Houghton Mifflin Harcourt Publishing Company • Image Credits: (t) ©Will Schmidt/YAY Micro/age fotostock; (b) ©Scott T. Smith/Corbis Documentary/Getty Images

Claims, Evidence, and Reasoning

Constructing an Argument

Constructing a strong argument is useful in science and engineering and in everyday life. A strong argument has three parts: a claim, evidence, and reasoning. Scientists and engineers use claims-evidence-reasoning arguments to communicate their explanations and solutions to others and to challenge or debate the conclusions of other scientists and engineers. The words *argue* and *argument* do not mean that scientists or engineers are fighting about something. Instead, this is a way to support a claim using evidence. Argumentation is a calm and rational way for people to examine all the facts and come to the best conclusion.

A **claim** is a statement that answers the question "What do you know?" A claim is a statement of your understanding of a phenomenon, answer to a question, or solution to a problem. A claim states what you think is true based on the information you have.

Evidence is any data that are related to your claim and answer the question "How do you know that?" These data may be from your own experiments and observations, reports by scientists or engineers, or other reliable data. Arguments made in science and engineering should be supported by empirical evidence. Empirical evidence is evidence that comes from observation or experiment.

Evidence used to support a claim should also be relevant and sufficient. Relevant evidence is evidence that is about the claim, and not about something else. Evidence is sufficient when there is enough evidence to fully support the claim.

Reasoning is the use of logical, analytical thought to form conclusions or inferences. Reasoning answers the question "Why does your evidence support your claim?" So, reasoning explains the relationship between your evidence and your claim. Reasoning might include a scientific law or principle that helps explain the relationship between the evidence and the claim.

Here is an example of a claims-evidence-reasoning argument.

Claim	Ice melts faster in the sun than it does in the shade.
Evidence	Two ice cubes of the same size were each placed in a plastic dish. One dish was placed on a wooden bench in the sun and one was placed on a different part of the same bench in the shade. The ice cube in the sun melted in 14 minutes and 32 seconds. The ice cube in the shade melted in 18 minutes and 15 seconds.
Reasoning	This experiment was designed so that the only variable that was different in the set-up of the two ice cubes was whether they were in the shade or in the sun. Because the ice cube in the sun melted almost 4 minutes faster than the one in the shade, this is sufficient evidence to say that ice melts faster in the sun than it does in the shade.

To summarize, a strong argument:

• presents a claim that is clear, logical, and well-defended
• supports the claim with empirical evidence that is sufficient and relevant
• includes reasons that make sense and are presented in a logical order

Constructing Your Own Argument

Now construct your own argument by recording a claim, evidence, and reasoning. With your teacher's permission, you can do an investigation to answer a question you have about how the world works. Or you can construct your argument based on observations you have already made about the world.

Claim	
Evidence	
Reasoning	

 For more information on claims, evidence, and reasoning, see the online **English Language Arts Handbook.**

Whether you are in the lab or in the field, you are responsible for your own safety and the safety of others. To fulfill these responsibilities and avoid accidents, be aware of the safety of your classmates as well as your own safety at all times. Take your lab work and fieldwork seriously, and behave appropriately. Elements of safety to keep in mind are shown below and on the following pages.

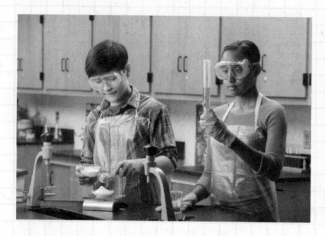

Safety in the Lab

- [ ] Be sure you understand the materials, your procedure, and the safety rules before you start an investigation in the lab.

- [ ] Know where to find and how to use fire extinguishers, eyewash stations, shower stations, and emergency power shutoffs.

- [ ] Use proper safety equipment. Always wear personal protective equipment, such as eye protection and gloves, when setting up labs, during labs, and when cleaning up.

- [ ] Do not begin until your teacher has told you to start. Follow directions.

- [ ] Keep the lab neat and uncluttered. Clean up when you are finished. Report all spills to your teacher immediately. Watch for slip/fall and trip/fall hazards.

- [ ] If you or another student is injured in any way, tell your teacher immediately, even if the injury seems minor.

- [ ] Do not take any food or drink into the lab. Never take any chemicals out of the lab.

Safety in the Field

- [ ] Be sure you understand the goal of your fieldwork and the proper way to carry out the investigation before you begin fieldwork.

- [ ] Use proper safety equipment and personal protective equipment, such as eye protection, that suits the terrain and the weather.

- [ ] Follow directions, including appropriate safety procedures as provided by your teacher.

- [ ] Do not approach or touch wild animals. Do not touch plants unless instructed by your teacher to do so. Leave natural areas as you found them.

- [ ] Stay with your group.

- [ ] Use proper accident procedures, and let your teacher know about a hazard in the environment or an accident immediately, even if the hazard or accident seems minor.

Safety Symbols

To highlight specific types of precautions, the following symbols are used throughout the lab program. Remember that no matter what safety symbols you see within each lab, all safety rules should be followed at all times.

Dress Code

- Wear safety goggles (or safety glasses as appropriate for the activity) at all times in the lab as directed. If chemicals get into your eye, flush your eyes immediately for a minimum of 15 minutes.
- Do not wear contact lenses in the lab.
- Do not look directly at the sun or any intense light source or laser.
- Wear appropriate protective non-latex gloves as directed.
- Wear an apron or lab coat at all times in the lab as directed.
- Tie back long hair, secure loose clothing, and remove loose jewelry. Remove acrylic nails when working with active flames.
- Do not wear open-toed shoes, sandals, or canvas shoes in the lab.

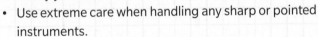

Glassware and Sharp Object Safety

- Do not use chipped or cracked glassware.
- Use heat-resistant glassware for heating or storing hot materials.
- Notify your teacher immediately if a piece of glass breaks.
- Use extreme care when handling any sharp or pointed instruments.
- Do not cut an object while holding the object unsupported in your hands. Place the object on a suitable cutting surface, and always cut in a direction away from your body.

Chemical Safety

- If a chemical gets on your skin, on your clothing, or in your eyes, rinse it immediately for a minimum of 15 minutes (using the shower, faucet, or eyewash station), and alert your teacher.
- Do not clean up spilled chemicals unless your teacher directs you to do so.
- Do not inhale any gas or vapor unless directed to do so by your teacher. If you are instructed to note the odor of a substance, wave the fumes toward your nose with your hand. This is called wafting. Never put your nose close to the source of the odor.
- Handle materials that emit vapors or gases in a well-ventilated area.
- Keep your hands away from your face while you are working on any activity.

Safety Symbols, continued

Electrical Safety

- Do not use equipment with frayed electrical cords or loose plugs.
- Do not use electrical equipment near water or when clothing or hands are wet.
- Hold the plug housing when you plug in or unplug equipment. Do not pull on the cord.
- Use only GFI-protected electrical receptacles.

Heating and Fire Safety

- Be aware of any source of flames, sparks, or heat (such as flames, heating coils, or hot plates) before working with any flammable substances.
- Know the location of the lab's fire extinguisher and fire-safety blankets.
- Know your school's fire-evacuation routes.
- If your clothing catches on fire, walk to the lab shower to put out the fire. Do not run.
- Never leave a hot plate unattended while it is turned on or while it is cooling.
- Use tongs or appropriately insulated holders when handling heated objects.
- Allow all equipment to cool before storing it.

Plant and Animal Safety

- Do not eat any part of a plant.
- Do not pick any wild plant unless your teacher instructs you to do so.
- Handle animals only as your teacher directs.
- Treat animals carefully and respectfully.
- Wash your hands thoroughly with soap and water after handling any plant or animal.

Cleanup

- Clean all work surfaces and protective equipment as directed by your teacher.
- Dispose of hazardous materials or sharp objects only as directed by your teacher.
- Wash your hands thoroughly with soap and water before you leave the lab or after any activity.

Name: _____   Date: _____

Student Safety Quiz

Circle the letter of the BEST answer.

1. Before starting an investigation or lab procedure, you should
   A. try an experiment of your own
   B. open all containers and packages
   C. read all directions and make sure you understand them
   D. handle all the equipment to become familiar with it

2. At the end of any activity you should
   A. wash your hands thoroughly with soap and water before leaving the lab
   B. cover your face with your hands
   C. put on your safety goggles
   D. leave hot plates switched on

3. If you get hurt or injured in any way, you should
   A. tell your teacher immediately
   B. find bandages or a first aid kit
   C. go to your principal's office
   D. get help after you finish the lab

4. If your glassware is chipped or broken, you should
   A. use it only for solid materials
   B. give it to your teacher for recycling or disposal
   C. put it back into the storage cabinet
   D. increase the damage so that it is obvious

5. If you have unused chemicals after finishing a procedure, you should
   A. pour them down a sink or drain
   B. mix them all together in a bucket
   C. put them back into their original containers
   D. dispose of them as directed by your teacher

6. If electrical equipment has a frayed cord, you should
   A. unplug the equipment by pulling the cord
   B. let the cord hang over the side of a counter or table
   C. tell your teacher about the problem immediately
   D. wrap tape around the cord to repair it

7. If you need to determine the odor of a chemical or a solution, you should
   A. use your hand to bring fumes from the container to your nose
   B. bring the container under your nose and inhale deeply
   C. tell your teacher immediately
   D. use odor-sensing equipment

8. When working with materials that might fly into the air and hurt someone's eye, you should wear
   A. goggles
   B. an apron
   C. gloves
   D. a hat

9. Before doing experiments involving a heat source, you should know the location of the
   A. door
   B. window
   C. fire extinguisher
   D. overhead lights

10. If you get chemicals in your eye you should
   A. wash your hands immediately
   B. put the lid back on the chemical container
   C. wait to see if your eye becomes irritated
   D. use the eyewash station right away, for a minimum of 15 minutes

Go online to view the Lab Safety Handbook for additional information.

XV

Earth's Surface and Society

How do natural processes and human activities affect Earth's surface and society?

Wildfires , such as this one in the Rocky Mountains, can destroy thousands of acres of forest and can threaten human cities and homes.

You Solve It Where and When Do Most Human-Caused Fires Occur? Analyze data about wildfires to decide when and where to run a public awareness campaign about preventing fires.

Go online and complete the You Solve It to explore ways to solve a real-world problem.

Develop a Natural Hazard Mitigation Plan

Students practice taking cover during an earthquake drill.

A. Look at the photo. On a separate sheet of paper, write down as many different questions as you can about the photo.

B. Discuss With your class or a partner, share your questions. Record any additional questions generated in your discussion. Then choose the most important questions from the list that are related to preparing for a natural hazard. Write them below.

C. Choose a natural hazard to research, and create a plan to minimize the effects of that hazard. Here's a list of natural hazards you can consider:

avalanche
blizzard or ice storm
cold wave
drought
earthquake

flood
hailstorm
hurricane or tropical cyclone
landslide
lightning or electrical storm

sinkhole
tornado or waterspout
tsunami
volcanic eruption
wildfire

D. Use the information on this page, along with your research, to explore how people prepare and respond to a natural hazard.

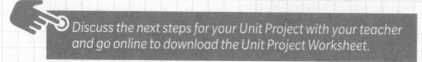

Discuss the next steps for your Unit Project with your teacher and go online to download the Unit Project Worksheet.

Language Development

Use the lessons in this unit to complete the network and expand your understanding of these key concepts.

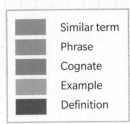

Similar term
Phrase
Cognate
Example
Definition

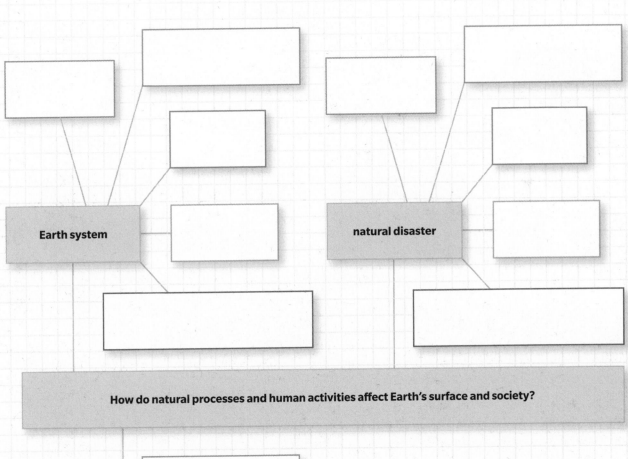

Earth system

natural disaster

How do natural processes and human activities affect Earth's surface and society?

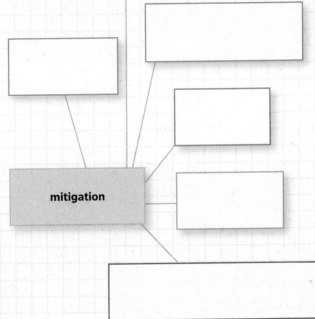

mitigation

Geologic Processes Change Earth's Surface

This mountain range in Banff National Park, Alberta, Canada, was formed by interactions among Earth's systems.

Explore First

Classifying Events Make a timeline of the events in your life. Use a key with symbols to indicate which of these events were large scale and which ones were small scale. Show which ones were short term, and which ones took longer. Compare your timeline with others'. Do any of your events overlap? Are they categorized in the same way?

Go online to view the digital version of the Hands-On Lab for this lesson and to download additional lab resources.

CAN YOU EXPLAIN IT?

How has this area of the Arizona desert changed in the last 50,000 years?

The Barringer Meteorite Crater is 1.3 km wide and extends 174 m into Earth. The crater formed about 50,000 years ago, when a meteorite with a mass of 300,000 metric tons hurtled through Earth's atmosphere nearly 50 times faster than a commercial jet. It struck Earth in what is now the Arizona Desert.

1. What immediate effects might the meteorite impact have had on Earth's surface?

2. Which changes might have happened after a longer time had passed?

EVIDENCE NOTEBOOK As you explore the lesson, gather evidence to help explain the changes to Earth's surface in this area over the last 50,000 years.

Analyzing Interactions Within the Earth System

The Earth System

A system is a group of related parts that work together as a whole. Earth itself is one large system, from its core to the outer edge of its atmosphere. The **Earth system** is all the matter, energy, and processes within this boundary. The Earth system is different from the systems of other planets and moons. Human survival depends on natural systems and cycles, as well as human-made systems. For example, food can only be grown in certain places at certain times. When humans disrupt natural systems and cycles, they also affect the ability of those systems to provide necessary resources, including food. As the human population increases, it has a growing influence on many of Earth's systems. Humans are using many resources at a faster rate than the resources can be replaced. As a result, many species are going extinct. The biodiversity that helps sustain stable Earth systems has been affected by human-made systems.

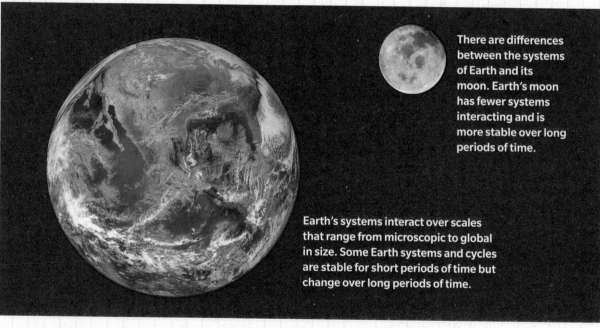

There are differences between the systems of Earth and its moon. Earth's moon has fewer systems interacting and is more stable over long periods of time.

Earth's systems interact over scales that range from microscopic to global in size. Some Earth systems and cycles are stable for short periods of time but change over long periods of time.

3. What difference or differences do you see between Earth and its moon? Put a check mark to show which statements are true for Earth and for the moon.

Earth	Moon	Statements
✓		Water covers much of the surface.
		The surface receives energy from the sun.
		It has a thick atmosphere and weather.
		The surface includes solid materials.
		Living organisms are visible on the surface.

Earth's Subsystems

The Earth system has many different parts that make up Earth's four major subsystems: the geosphere, hydrosphere, atmosphere, and biosphere. Many of Earth's materials are part of more than one subsystem. For example, fog is part of the atmosphere and the hydrosphere. These subsystems change over time, but also have periods of stability.

The interactions between Earth's subsystems happen over time spans that range from fractions of a second to billions of years. These interactions have shaped Earth's history. Earth's future will continue to be determined by these interactions as well as the decisions humans make about natural systems and resource use.

Earth's Subsystems

Atmosphere
The atmosphere is the part of the Earth system that includes all of the gases in a layer that surrounds Earth. Earth's weather and climate result from interactions between the parts of this subsystem. Human influences are affecting the long term stability of Earth's weather and climate systems.

Geosphere
The geosphere is the part of the Earth system that includes all of the rocks, minerals, and landforms on Earth's surface and all the matter in Earth's interior. The geosphere usually changes slowly and so it appears stable.

Biosphere
The biosphere is the part of the Earth system that includes all living organisms, from the smallest bacterium to the largest tree. The biosphere is constantly changing as organisms migrate, evolve, or become extinct.

Hydrosphere
The hydrosphere is the part of the Earth system that includes all Earth's water that is cycling between the surface, underground, or the atmosphere. The hydrosphere includes liquid water, water vapor, and the solid water in ice and snow.

EVIDENCE NOTEBOOK

4. Which of Earth's subsystems was most obviously affected by the meteorite impact? What changes occurred in that subsystem? Record your evidence.

5. Label each image with the appropriate subsystem. Some images may be labeled with more than one subsystem.

- geosphere
- biosphere
- atmosphere
- hydrosphere

_____   _____   _____

6. Discuss How do you use resources from each of Earth's four subsystems on any given day?

The Cycling of Matter and Energy

Earth's subsystems constantly interact, and as they do, energy and matter cycle through the Earth system. Energy and matter also cycle between natural systems and human-made systems. Natural and human-made systems are dependent on each other and can affect each other over both short and long periods of time.

Energy from the sun and from Earth's interior is transferred by several processes, including wind, water waves, and movements of rock. In fact, energy from the sun is one of the main drivers of erosion and deposition. Interactions between the hydrosphere and the atmosphere also drive weather and climate systems. While the climate of a region may stay stable for decades, seasonal differences in solar radiation result in changes in weather throughout the year.

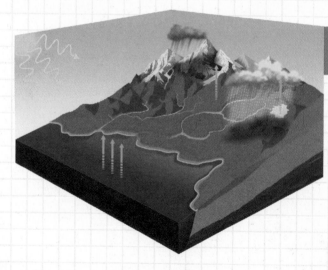

Explore Online

Energy from the sun drives interactions between subsystems on Earth's surface.

_____

7. _____ causes rain to fall to Earth's surface. Energy from _____ causes water to evaporate.

Energy from Earth's Interior

Energy from Earth's interior is transferred upward through Earth's layers. Several processes transfer energy and matter through the geosphere. For example, hot magma in Earth's upper mantle and lower crust can rise to the surface in a volcanic eruption. The eruption can cause heat and small particles of rock and minerals from deep within Earth's crust to enter the atmosphere. The energy and matter from the eruption can kill organisms and destroy habitats, causing stable ecosystems to change very quickly. Hot ash and lava can heat the water in streams or lakes, sometimes changing liquid water into steam. The eruption also brings minerals from within Earth to its surface, where they can be used by organisms. Other energy transfers from Earth's interior cause the melting of rock, earthquakes, and the movement of Earth's plates.

8. The rocks that make up Earth's interior and surface melt and form

_____,

which pushes up through rock to form volcanoes. Volcanoes underwater release energy from Earth's interior into the

_____.

Energy from Earth's interior causes the movement of tectonic plates and the formation of volcanoes. These movements affect all four of Earth's subsystems.

Explain Earth Systems Interactions

The interactions among Earth's subsystems are often quite complex. A single event, such as a forest fire, results in the cycling of energy and matter among the systems in many different ways. Effects on the subsystems can be positive, negative, or both.

9. **Discuss** Together with a partner, study the scene shown in the photograph. Describe subsystem interactions you can infer from the scene and explain the cycling of matter and energy that could be occurring with each interaction.

A forest fire can affect more than just the biosphere.

_____

_____

_____

_____

_____

_____

Explaining the Changes on Earth's Surface

Some changes to Earth's surface are easy to see—they are big changes that happen quickly, such as a landslide. Other changes can start out small and occur slowly but become big changes over many years. An example is the erosion of Earth's mountains. The changes to Earth's surface—big or small, fast or slow—are the result of Earth's subsystems interacting.

10. **Discuss** Together with a partner, examine the photo of the cone-shaped deposit. Did this deposit form recently, or did it form many years ago? What evidence do you observe to support your answer?

This cone-shaped deposit of sediment is caused by the deposition of sediment and rock where a stream leaves a narrow channel such as a canyon and spreads out in a wider area such as a plain.

Large-Scale and Small-Scale Changes

Most changes on Earth's surface are the result of interactions of Earth's subsystems. Changes on Earth's surface range from microscopic to global in scale. A smaller-scale change may be crystal formation, while ocean shore erosion is a larger-scale change. Global-sized changes, such as movements of Earth's tectonic plates, affect all of Earth.

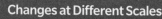

Changes at Different Scales

Larger-scale changes happen when the plates in Earth's crust move slowly as the mantle beneath them moves. Plate motion squeezes, stretches, and breaks Earth's crust. These motions slowly shape global-scale features, such as wide ocean basins, deep ocean trenches, and long mountain chains, like the Himalayas pictured here.

Smaller-scale changes happen when oxygen and water chemically react with minerals in rocks. These reactions cause the rocks to change and break down. Similarly, organisms that live on rocks, such as lichen, produce chemicals that cause rocks to break down. These changes affect much smaller areas on Earth's surface.

11. The events listed below describe changes to Earth's surface. Classify the changes as smaller-scale, medium-scale, or larger-scale by writing the correct label on the line next to each event. Assign each scale to only two events.

> **WORD BANK**
> • smaller-scale change
> • medium-scale change
> • larger-scale change

A. Water and ice weather and erode a rock.

smaller-scale change

B. Two plates collide, causing a mountain range to form.

_____

C. Heavy rainfall causes a landslide.

_____

D. An oil spill damages a coastal ecosystem.

_____

E. Gravity causes a rock structure on a beach to collapse into the ocean.

_____

F. A plant dies and decays, and its nutrients become part of the soil.

_____

EVIDENCE NOTEBOOK

12. How would you classify the scale of the change to Earth's surface due to the impact of the meteorite? Provide evidence to support your answer.

Time Scales of Changes

Geologic processes happen on varying time scales. Some events that change Earth's surface happen very quickly, such as erosion and deposition caused by floods. Other processes happen slowly, such as the growth of cave formations caused by groundwater. The processes may take so long, in fact, that we may think nothing is happening. When wind, water, and ice cause erosion and deposition over a long time scale, mountains and valleys form. However, because these changes sometimes occur over millions or billions of years, humans usually can observe only a small part of most processes that change Earth's surface. The geosphere usually appears very stable.

The same processes that shaped Earth's surface in the past continue to shape Earth's surface today. Some of these processes may have occurred more often or less often in the past than they do today. An example is the large meteorites that impacted Earth early in its history. Meteorite impacts occur much less frequently today.

Do the Math

Compare Rates of Change

Changes on Earth's surface happen at many different rates. Both rapid and slow processes can cause changes to landforms on Earth's surface. For example, plate movement can trigger earthquakes, which happen suddenly. As plates move, continents can break apart and mountain ranges can form over millions of years. Three changes that usually happen at different rates are:

- flow of a fast glacier (17 km/year)
- spreading at the Mid-Atlantic Ridge (2 cm/year)
- formation of a stalactite in a cave (3 mm/year)

The dark gray area is the Mid-Atlantic Ridge in the Atlantic Ocean.

13. In the table below, use what you know about the original rate data to complete the order column by ranking the processes as fastest or slowest.

Process	Original Data	Order	Converted Data
glacier flow	17 km/year		
sea-floor spreading	2 cm/year	middle	2 cm/year
stalactite formation	3 mm/year		

14. Complete the converted data column by converting all the rates to cm/year. Remember: 1 km = 100,000 cm and 1 cm = 10 mm

15. What is the difference between comparing the rates using the original rate data and the data converted to cm/year? Which data set is easier to use to compare the rates of change? Explain your reasoning.

16. **Engineer It** How could you measure the speed of a glacier if it takes a year to move several kilometers? What is one additional challenge scientists face in measuring the spreading rate at a mid-ocean ridge compared to measuring the speed of a glacier?

Fast and Slow Changes

Earth's surface has been changing over billions of years. Many of the changes happen in a matter of minutes, while others may take millions of years to occur. As you look at events that change Earth's surface, comparisons can be made to give you a sense of these time scales. For example, you can compare two events—the formation of a river delta and a river flooding—that can occur in your lifetime. A river delta forms when sediments carried by a river are deposited where it empties into the ocean. A river delta might grow slowly each day, with changes visible in a couple of months or a year's time. In comparison, floods may occur when there is heavy rainfall in a short period of time. This can cause lakes and rivers to overflow and flood the surrounding area. Humans can influence the rate at which many changes occur. For example, building a dam along a river changes cycles of flooding. This may benefit farmers by controlling the flow of water, but may harm ecosystems downstream. Humans can build a dam quickly, but both Earth and human systems will be changed for a long time.

This river delta formed from sediments deposited by the river that flows into the sea here.

The level of this river is higher than normal. It can erode sediment and other materials, depositing them in new locations in a matter of hours, days, or weeks.

17. Relative to a human lifetime, delta formation is a large, slow / fast process that involves small / medium / large amounts of energy and matter over a longer time. A flash flood is a slow / fast process that involves small / large amounts of energy and matter over a shorter time.

EVIDENCE NOTEBOOK

18. When the meteorite hit Earth in Arizona, did its impact cause fast or slow changes to Earth's surface? Support your claim with evidence.

Hands-On Lab
Analyze Visual Evidence

What changes can a volcanic eruption cause? You will use maps to analyze the visible changes to the Mount St. Helens area that were caused by a powerful eruption.

MATERIALS
• colored pencils

The eruption of Mount St. Helens, a volcanic mountain in the Cascade Range in the state of Washington, is an example of a rapid change that caused medium-scale changes to Earth's surface.

The volcano had been dormant since 1857, but on the morning of May 18, 1980, a massive earthquake (magnitude 5.1 on the Richter scale) caused the volcano's north side to collapse. An avalanche of rock fell onto the land below. Then gases that had been under pressure inside the mountain shot out sideways, destroying 500 km² of surrounding forest. Ash rose thousands of feet into the air, and pyroclastic flows streamed down the mountain's sides. After nine hours, the eruption was over, but Earth's surface in the area was dramatically changed.

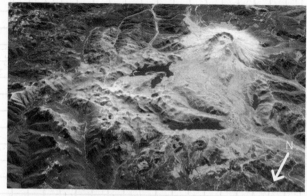

This satellite image of Mount St. Helens was taken after the eruption in 1980.

Procedure and Analysis

STEP 1 In this activity, you are provided with information about Mount St. Helens and two maps of the area. One map is from the time between 1970 and 1980, before the eruption. The other map is from 1980, after the eruption.

STEP 2 Compare the two maps. Look for differences between them. What changed in the area around Mount St. Helens after the eruption?

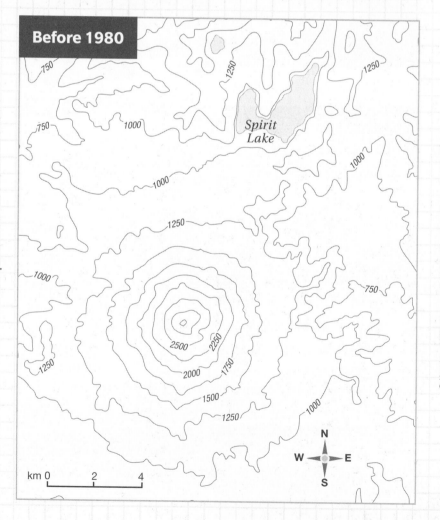

Before 1980

© Houghton Mifflin Harcourt Publishing Company • Image Credits: ©NASA Earth Observatory image by Jesse Allen and Joshua Stevens, using Landsat data from the USGS

STEP 3 From among your observations, choose something that changed after the eruption. Use the colored pencils to indicate the feature on the "before" map and where it has changed on the "after" map. Outline or color the feature in a way that makes it clear to a viewer what feature you are highlighting.

STEP 4 Choose at least two other changes and mark your maps to show them.

STEP 5 Create a map legend that explains the colors and their meanings.

STEP 6 Based on evidence from the maps, which statement describes Mount St. Helens after the changes occurred as a result of the eruption? Circle all that apply.

    A. The shape of Spirit Lake was not affected by the eruption.

    B. The land south of Mount St. Helens was changed more than the land to the north.

    C. The eruption caused the erosion and deposition of rocks and sediment.

    D. The eruption left a large crater on Mount St. Helens that reduced the overall height of the mountain.

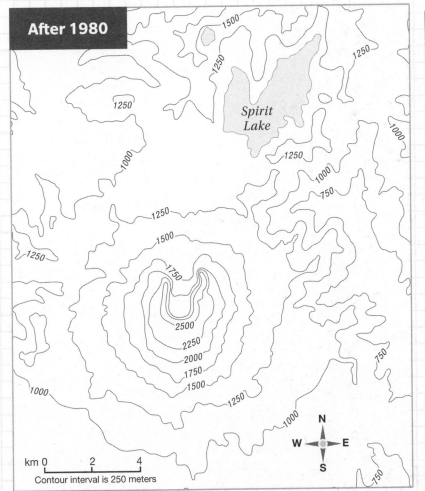

Examine Changes over Time

This volcanic rock has been sitting on the coastline of Maui, Hawaii, for many years. The rock, a result of cooled lava, has changed over time.

19. Study the photograph of the volcanic rock. Do you think the rocks have always looked like this? Provide evidence to support your answer.

_____

_____

_____

_____

_____

20. Write Compose a story about the fast and slow changes that caused the rock in the photograph to look the way it does today.

_____

_____

_____

_____

_____

_____

_____

_____

_____

_____

Continue Your Exploration

Name: _____   **Date:** _____

Check out the path below or go online to choose one of the other paths shown.

> **Geologically Active Yellowstone**

- **Destination Mars**
- **Hands-On Labs** 🖐
- **Propose Your Own Path**

Go online to choose one of these other paths.

Yellowstone National Park covers parts of Wyoming, Montana, and Idaho. About 640,000 years ago, magma in a chamber below the surface pushed Earth's crust up, creating a dome. A huge volcanic explosion emptied the magma chamber. The dome cracked and collapsed, forming the Yellowstone Caldera. A caldera is a depression formed when a magma chamber below a volcano empties.

Today, there is still a magma chamber below the Yellowstone Caldera. In some places it is less than 10 km below the surface. About 9% of the chamber is molten rock, or magma, found in small pockets within very hot solid rock. There are also many fractures and faults, or breaks in rock, in and around the caldera. When rocks move along a fault and release energy, earthquakes occur. Many earthquakes happen near the Yellowstone Caldera.

Yellowstone National Park also contains about 10,000 hydrothermal features, such as geysers and hot springs. The energy source for all these features is the magma chamber below the Yellowstone Caldera. If water flows through or over hot rock, it can become very hot or even turn into steam. Hot springs are places where hot groundwater rises to Earth's surface. Geysers are hot springs where water and steam erupt periodically from surface pools or small vents. The geyser eruption empties an underground chamber where the water had collected. The chamber then refills with groundwater and erupts again after the water is hot enough to boil.

1. Describe an interaction between Earth's subsystems that is happening in Yellowstone National Park today. Describe the cycling of matter and flow of energy involved in this interaction.

A geyser erupts at Yellowstone National Park.

Continue Your Exploration

Cutaway Diagram of the Yellowstone Caldera Area

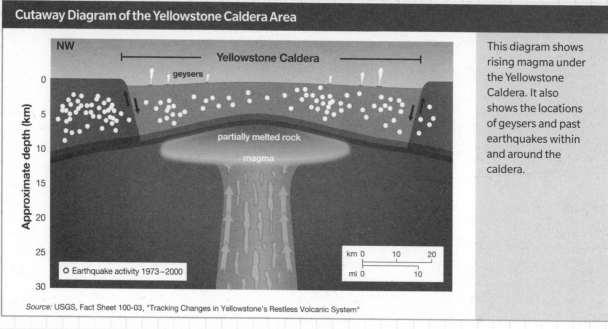

This diagram shows rising magma under the Yellowstone Caldera. It also shows the locations of geysers and past earthquakes within and around the caldera.

Source: USGS, Fact Sheet 100-03, "Tracking Changes in Yellowstone's Restless Volcanic System"

2. There are large faults at the edges of the Yellowstone Caldera. The caldera formed when the magma chamber emptied. How do the movement arrows on the faults in the diagram explain what happened when the caldera formed?

3. Describe the locations of the geysers in this diagram. Develop an explanation for why the geysers are found inside of and not outside of the caldera.

4. **Collaborate** Discuss with a classmate how Earth's surface may change in Yellowstone over the next 100 years. What features may be affected? Provide evidence from the image to support your argument.

Can You Explain It?

Name: _____ Date: _____

How has this area of the Arizona desert changed in the last 50,000 years?

EVIDENCE NOTEBOOK

Refer to the notes in your Evidence Notebook to help you identify the immediate effects of the meteorite on Earth's systems, as well as the changes that were observed over time.

1. State your claim. Make sure your claim fully explains how this area of the Arizona desert has changed over the last 50,000 years.

2. Summarize the evidence you have gathered to support your claim and explain your reasoning.

Checkpoints

Answer the following questions to check your understanding of the lesson.

Use the photo to answer Questions 3–4.

3. Which phrases apply to the formation of the Grand Canyon? Select all that apply.

   A. medium scale

   B. long-term

   C. small scale

   D. short-term

   E. large scale

4. What is the primary source of energy that drove the cycling of matter that formed the Grand Canyon?

   A. the sun

   B. weathering

   C. erosion

Use the photo to answer Questions 5–6.

5. This photo shows evidence of the interaction of Earth's subsystems. Which of Earth's subsystems are interacting during a landslide? Select all that apply.

   A. geosphere

   B. biosphere

   C. atmosphere

   D. hydrosphere

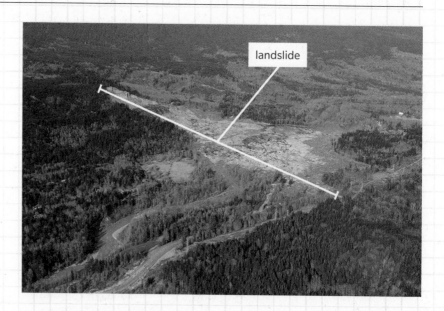

landslide

6. The devastation from the landslide shown—the disturbed soil, the knocked-over trees, the blocked waterway and road—are evidence that the change happened rapidly / slowly over time.

Interactive Review

Complete this section to review the main concepts of the lesson.

Earth's subsystems are the geosphere, atmosphere, hydrosphere, and biosphere. Energy and matter are transferred when Earth's subsystems interact with each other and with human-made systems.

A. Describe which of Earth's subsystems are involved when an oil spill occurs in a coastal ecosystem. Explain how these different subsystems may be affected over a long period of time.

Geologic processes change Earth's surface on varying scales of space and time. They range from rapid to very slow; from global to microscopic. Humans can also change Earth's surface and speed up or slow down some geologic processes.

B. How can humans change the time scale at which some geologic processes take place when a dam is built along a river?

Natural Hazards Disrupt Earth's Surface

In 2015, this wildfire near Clear Lake, California, destroyed property and devastated the environment.

Explore First

Modeling a Sandstorm Spread a cup of sand evenly in the bottom of an open top shoe box. From a distance of about one meter, blow air from a hairdryer towards the sand in the box. What happens to the sand in the box? How might this process affect Earth's surface?

Go online to view the digital version of the Hands-On Lab for this lesson and to download additional lab resources.

CAN YOU EXPLAIN IT?

How was this city suddenly buried without warning?

In the 1700s, scientists in Italy discovered a city that had been buried for over 1,900 years. As they dug down to see more and more of the city, it appeared that the city had been buried very suddenly. They discovered that the buildings and other structures were still standing, and there were cavities in the ground in the shapes of people and animals all over the city. The city's inhabitants had been buried suddenly, and over hundreds of years the bodies had decayed. Scientists began filling the cavities with plaster or cement and letting it dry. Then they carefully removed the material around the cement so they could see the shape of the cavity. One of these cement casts is shown in the photo.

1. What could have buried this city and its inhabitants so suddenly?

EVIDENCE NOTEBOOK As you explore this lesson, gather evidence to help explain what could have suddenly buried this ancient city.

Describing Natural Hazards and Natural Disasters

A naturally occurring event that can have a negative effect on humans or the environment is called a **natural hazard**. Natural hazards include floods, storms, droughts, avalanches, wildfires, earthquakes, tsunamis, hurricanes, tornadoes, and volcanic eruptions. Natural hazards also include the spread of disease and space-related hazards, such as meteorite impacts. Humans cannot control the causes of natural hazards, but some human activities may influence the intensity and frequency of some natural hazards. Understanding these events can help humans find ways to make these events less destructive. Humans can identify areas where natural hazards are likely to occur and find ways to prepare for these events.

Natural Hazard Risk in the United States

This map shows where the risk is greatest for tornadoes, hurricanes, and earthquakes.

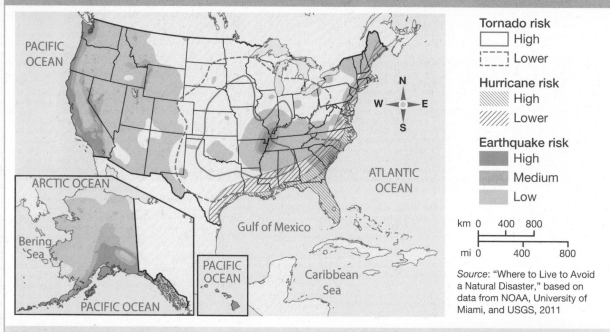

Tornado risk
High
Lower

Hurricane risk
High
Lower

Earthquake risk
High
Medium
Low

km 0   400   800
mi 0   400   800

Source: "Where to Live to Avoid a Natural Disaster," based on data from NOAA, University of Miami, and USGS, 2011

Earthquakes are sudden, short-term, geologic events in which the ground shakes violently.

Hurricanes are massive storms that are characterized by high winds, heavy rain, and coastal flooding.

Tornadoes are weather events that involve strong, rotating winds and may involve hail and rain.

2. **Discuss** Do any of the natural hazards shown on the map occur where you live? Do you know why or why not? Discuss your ideas with a partner.

Natural Hazards and Natural Disasters

Any natural hazard can become a **natural disaster** if it causes widespread injury, death, property damage, or damage to an ecosystem. A natural disaster may occur in only one small area, or it may cover large areas—even several countries. As the human population increases, the number of natural disasters increases as well. Whenever a natural hazard affects a heavily populated area, the chance of it becoming a natural disaster increases. For example, a heavy rain that would soak into the ground may cause a flood in an area that has been covered in roads and buildings.

3. Label each photo to show whether it is a natural hazard or a natural disaster.

Sometimes, hurricanes occur over the ocean and never reach land. This satellite image shows several large hurricanes. Hawaii is in the middle of the image.
_____

Hurricanes with strong winds and heavy rain can cause flooding and structural damage if they reach land. This photo shows Hurricane Isaac when it struck Gulfport, Mississippi, in 2012.
_____

Types of Natural Hazards

There are many types of natural hazards. Weather hazards include thunderstorms, tropical storms, lightning, and tornadoes. Too much rain can cause floods, erosion, and landslides. Too little rain can cause droughts, which are climate hazards that can disrupt ecosystems. Geologic hazards include earthquakes and volcanic eruptions. Earthquakes can cause ground shaking, landslides, and tsunamis. Volcanic eruptions can bring molten rock, hot gases, and volcanic ash to Earth's surface. Other types of natural hazards include wildfires, space-related hazards such as asteroid impacts, and widespread diseases. Sometimes natural hazards are related to each other. For example, an area is more likely to have wildfires during a drought. Earthquakes can cause tsunamis that rapidly flood coastal areas.

Worldwide Natural Disasters, 1995–2015		
Natural hazard type	Number of occurrences	Percentage of total (%)
Flood	3,062	43
Storm	2,018	28
Earthquake	562	8
Extreme temperature	405	6
Landslide	387	5
Drought	334	5
Wildfire	251	3
Volcanic eruption	111	2

Source: The Centre for Research on the Epidemiology of Disasters, United Nations Office for Disaster Risk Reduction, *The Human Cost of Weather Related Disasters, 1995–2015*

4. **Draw** Create a circle graph or another type of graphic to show what percentage of all worldwide natural disasters each hazard type represents.

Geologic Hazards

Geologic hazards are caused by geologic processes such as tectonic plate motion or erosion. Some geologic hazards, such as landslides, earthquakes, tsunamis, and volcanic eruptions, can happen quickly or without warning.

When groundwater dissolves rock below the surface, the ground can suddenly collapse to form a *sinkhole*.

Earthquakes occur when slabs of Earth's crust move and release energy, causing violent shaking.

A *tsunami* is a powerful wave caused by movement of ocean water after an earthquake, a landslide, or an eruption.

Weather and Climate Hazards

Weather describes the conditions in the atmosphere at any given time. *Climate* describes long-term weather patterns. Weather and climate hazards include droughts, hurricanes, tornadoes, blizzards, severe thunderstorms, and floods. Severe storms can have heavy rain, lightning, high winds, and hail, and they can lead to tornadoes and floods.

When heavy rain cannot soak into the ground it runs over Earth's surface and causes a *flood*.

During a *drought*, too little rain causes the land to dry out, and plants are unable to get the water they need.

Very cold temperatures and strong winds combined with extreme amounts of snowfall cause a *blizzard*.

EVIDENCE NOTEBOOK

5. What kinds of natural hazards could suddenly bury a city and the people who live there? Record your evidence.

Natural Hazard Data

Historical data from past natural hazards help us understand the causes and effects of natural hazards and allow us to see patterns in hazard occurrences. Depending on the natural hazard, data could include location, time, and duration. It may also include *frequency*, or how often events occur, and *magnitude*, or how large events are. These data help researchers identify how human activity may affect the magnitude and frequency of some natural hazards. Current conditions are also monitored to learn about natural hazards. For example, weather instruments collect data on current atmospheric conditions. Meteorologists analyze these data to determine when and where a storm might occur.

6. **Discuss** Look at the data in the two maps. Is there a correlation between historic earthquake locations and earthquake hazard level?

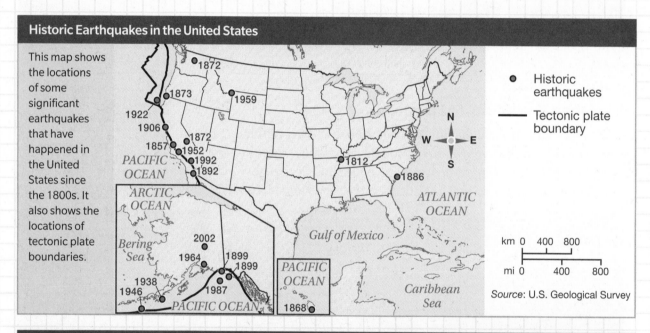

Historic Earthquakes in the United States

This map shows the locations of some significant earthquakes that have happened in the United States since the 1800s. It also shows the locations of tectonic plate boundaries.

Source: U.S. Geological Survey

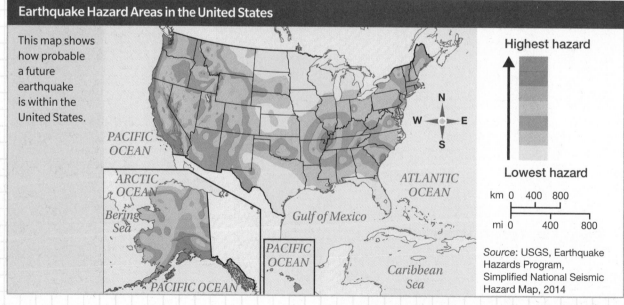

Earthquake Hazard Areas in the United States

This map shows how probable a future earthquake is within the United States.

Source: USGS, Earthquake Hazards Program, Simplified National Seismic Hazard Map, 2014

Do the Math
Interpret Natural Disaster Data

The table shows the number of people affected by weather and climate disasters.

Effects of Weather and Climate Disasters Worldwide, 1995–2015	
Natural hazard type	**Number of people affected (excluding deaths)**
Flood	2,300,000,000
Drought	1,100,000,000
Storm	660,000,000
Extreme temperatures	94,000,000
Landslide and wildfire	8,000,000

Source: The Centre for Research on the Epidemiology of Disasters, United Nations Office for Disaster Risk Reduction, *The Human Cost of Weather Related Disasters, 1995–2015*

7. One researcher claimed, "Between 1995 and 2015, more than twice as many people were affected by floods as were affected by all of the other natural hazard types combined."

   STEP 1 Use the variables to write an expression to represent the researcher's claim. You can divide the number of people affected by floods by the total number of people affected by other natural hazard types.

   f = number affected by floods

   a = number affected by all other natural hazard types combined

   $$\frac{number\ affected\ by\ floods}{(number\ affected\ by\ other\ natural\ hazard\ types)} = \underline{\quad\quad\quad}$$

   STEP 2 Simplify the expression by dividing. Round to the nearest hundredth.

   STEP 3 Do the data support the researcher's claim? Explain.

8. Based on your results, do you think the researcher should reword the claim? Explain.

Interpreting Patterns in Volcanic Data

A *volcano* is a place where molten rock and gases can rise from Earth's interior to the surface. Volcanoes are located on continents and at the bottom of the ocean. Some volcanoes are tall mountains, while others are just cracks in Earth's surface. A *volcanic eruption* is a geologic hazard in which molten rock—called *magma* or *lava*—gases, ash, and other materials are released onto Earth's surface and into the atmosphere.

9. Match these terms to the photos: explosive, quiet.

Explore Online

A. During _____ eruptions, lava oozes downhill.

B. During _____ eruptions, lava, ash, and gases shoot into the air.

Volcanic Eruptions

When a volcano erupts, molten rock reaches Earth's surface. Once at the surface, the molten rock is called *lava*. Not all volcanic eruptions are the same. Some are explosive, forcefully throwing hot lava, ash, and gases into the air. Volcanic eruptions may also be quiet or slow, with lava oozing out and flowing downhill.

Volcanoes erupt on Earth every day, but most eruptions are small or far from human populations. Only some of Earth's volcanoes have erupted in the past 10,000 years. These are considered *active volcanoes*. Those that have not erupted in the past 10,000 years are considered *dormant volcanoes*. If geologists agree that a volcano is not likely to erupt ever again, it is considered an *extinct volcano*.

Volcano Classification and Volcanic Hazards

Volcanic eruptions are natural disasters when they cause property damage, injury, or death. Lava flows can burn down structures and start wildfires. Gases can cause breathing issues. A dense cloud of hot ash over 1,000 °C can flow along the ground. This is called a *pyroclastic flow*. Heat from volcanoes can melt ice and snow and form a mudflow called a *lahar*. Both pyroclastic flows and lahars move rapidly downhill and disrupt ecosystems. Ash from explosive eruptions can be spread by wind in the atmosphere and partially block sunlight, lowering Earth's temperature over a period of months to years. Volcanic ash can also contaminate water supplies. Large eruptions may cause earthquakes and tsunamis. Shaking from earthquakes can damage buildings and roads. *Tsunamis* are powerful ocean waves that can flood coastal areas.

Volcanic Explosivity Index (VEI)			
VEI number	Type of eruption	Minimum volume of material erupted (cubic kilometers, km³)	Eruption cloud height (km)
0	nonexplosive	0.000001	<0.1
1	gentle	0.00001	0.1–1
2	explosive	0.001	1–5
3	severe	0.01	3–15
4	cataclysmic	0.1	10–25
5	paroxysmal	1	>25
6	colossal	10	>25
7	super-colossal	100	>25
8	mega-colossal	1,000	>25

Scientists compare the magnitudes of volcanic eruptions by using the Volcanic Explosivity Index (VEI). The scale starts at 0 and has no upper limit. The largest known eruption had a magnitude of 8.

Source: USGS, "How Big Are Eruptions?" 2017

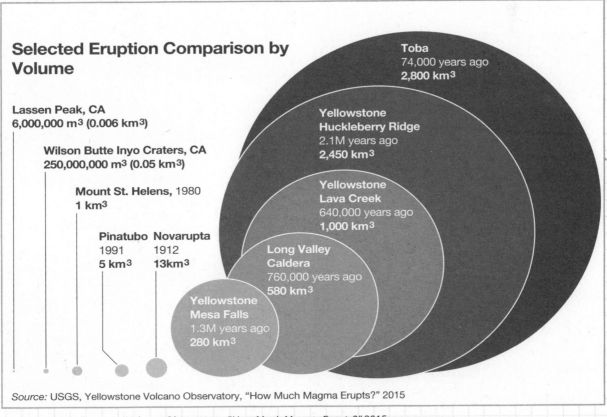

Selected Eruption Comparison by Volume

Lassen Peak, CA
6,000,000 m³ (0.006 km³)

Wilson Butte Inyo Craters, CA
250,000,000 m³ (0.05 km³)

Mount St. Helens, 1980
1 km³

Pinatubo 1991
5 km³

Novarupta 1912
13km³

Toba
74,000 years ago
2,800 km³

Yellowstone Huckleberry Ridge
2.1M years ago
2,450 km³

Yellowstone Lava Creek
640,000 years ago
1,000 km³

Long Valley Caldera
760,000 years ago
580 km³

Yellowstone Mesa Falls
1.3M years ago
280 km³

Source: USGS, Yellowstone Volcano Observatory, "How Much Magma Erupts?" 2015

Source: USGS, Yellowstone Volcano Observatory, "How Much Magma Erupts?" 2015

10. Use the table and the chart to complete the sentence. Mount Pinatubo erupted in 1991, as a(n) _____ on the VEI and is therefore categorized as a(n) _____ eruption.

Volcanic Hazards

The diagram and photos illustrate some of the hazards associated with a volcanic eruption.

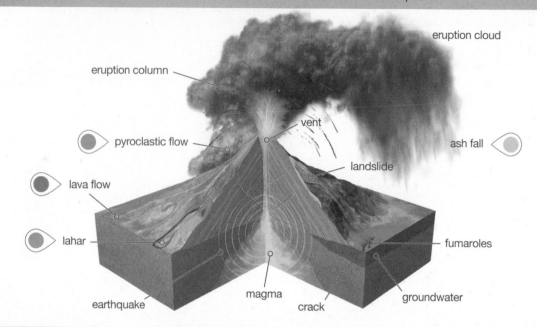

eruption cloud

eruption column

vent

pyroclastic flow

ash fall

lava flow

landslide

lahar

fumaroles

earthquake

magma

crack

groundwater

A *pyroclastic flow* can travel at speeds of up to 700 km/h and kill or destroy everything in its path. It may take many years for the local ecosystem to recover.

A *lahar* is a mudslide that is like a flood of concrete. A lahar can travel at speeds up to 200 km/h and can crush or carry away everything in its path.

Lava can surround and cover objects in its path. When lava cools, the objects are buried under hardened rock. Lava can flow at speeds up to 60 km/h and can also trigger wildfires.

As volcanic ash falls from the sky for hours to weeks after an eruption, it can bury everything, including buildings, homes, forests, and crops.

EVIDENCE NOTEBOOK

11. Could a volcanic eruption suddenly bury a city and its inhabitants? Record your evidence.

© Houghton Mifflin Harcourt Publishing Company • Image Credits: (tl) ©Y. T. Haryono/

Assess Building Sites Near a Volcano

You will assess potential building sites near an active volcano.

Kilauea (kee•low•AY•uh) volcano, located on the Big Island of Hawaii, has been erupting constantly since 1983. Lava has been continually flowing out of vents, or cracks, on the side of the volcano. Depending on where the lava is flowing from and the shape of the land it flows over, the direction of the lava flow changes. The volume of lava can also change.

Lava Flows on Kilauea

This map shows the locations of all the lava flows on Kilauea from 1983 to 2016. Much of the area is tropical rainforest. The white areas represent roads and communities.

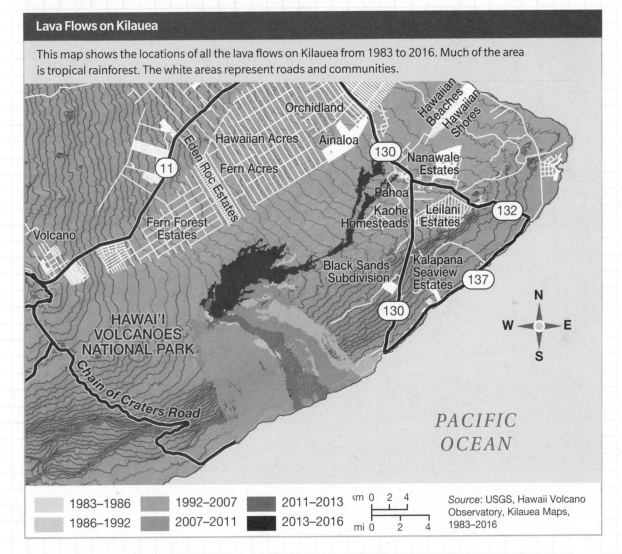

| | 1983–1986 | | 1992–2007 | | 2011–2013 | km 0 2 4 | Source: USGS, Hawaii Volcano |
| | 1986–1992 | | 2007–2011 | | 2013–2016 | mi 0 2 4 | Observatory, Kilauea Maps, 1983–2016 |

Procedure and Analysis

STEP 1 Use the map to identify where and when past lava flows occurred.

STEP 2 In the past, Kilauea has had many devastating and deadly eruptions. Today, the eruption of Kilauea is quiet rather than explosive. Hazards associated with the current type of eruption of Kilauea include poisonous _____ around the crater, _____ that burn vegetation and structures, and _____ that flows downhill.

WORD BANK
- wildfires
- lava
- gases

Engineer It

STEP 3 Imagine that a developer wants to build a hotel near the national park. What factors should the developer consider when deciding where to build? How would these factors affect where the hotel is built?

These homes near the town of Pahoa were destroyed by lava flowing from Kilauea in 2014.

STEP 4 Use the map to identify the best places to build the hotel. Select a building site that would be at a relatively low risk from the hazards of the volcano. Describe its location on the map.

STEP 5 Describe why you chose this site. Provide evidence from your knowledge of eruptions and from the map to describe why this site is the best choice.

Do the Math
Analyze Eruption Data

Although every volcanic eruption is different, scientists can compare the explosiveness, frequency, and size of volcanic eruptions. The table compares eruption size to eruption frequency and provides examples of volcanoes that fall into each category.

Mount Vesuvius, on the coast of Italy, has produced eight major eruptions within the last 17,000 years. These eruptions have included lava, pyroclastic flows, and ash clouds.

Volcanic Eruption Frequency and Size		
Eruption size (km^3)	Eruption frequency (approximate)	Volcano example(s)
< 0.001	Daily	Kilauea, Stromboli
0.001–0.01	Weekly to monthly	Etna
0.01–1	Annually	St. Helens (1980)
1–10	Once every 10 to 100 years	Pinatubo (1991), Vesuvius (79)
10–100	Once every 100 to 1,000 years	Krakatau (1883), Katmai (1912)
100–1,000	Once every 1,000 to 10,000 years	Tambora (1815)
> 1,000	Once or twice every 100,000 years	Yellowstone, Toba

Source: USGS, "How Big Are Eruptions?" 2017

12. Look at the table. Eruption size is the volume of material erupted. Eruption frequency is approximately how often an eruption of that size occurs. How would you describe the relationship between eruption size and eruption frequency?

_____

_____

_____

_____

_____

_____

Interpreting Patterns in Tornado Data

A *tornado* is a rapidly spinning column of air extending from a storm cloud to the ground. Tornadoes are weather hazards that are most common in spring and summer. This time of year is sometimes referred to as "tornado season."

This mobile Doppler radar truck was used to collect data from a storm in Nebraska that caused several tornadoes like the one shown in the inset. These data help scientists better understand how, when, and where tornadoes form and end.

Tornadoes

Severe thunderstorms can bring heavy rain, hail, high winds—and tornadoes. Tornadoes can develop when rotating thunderstorms, called *supercells*, occur. However, not all supercells form tornadoes. A combination of factors must be present for a tornado to form. A body of warm, moist air must collide with a body of cooler, drier air. As a result, winds at different altitudes blow at different speeds and cause a column of air in the thunderstorm to spin. Because the air pressure is low in the middle of the spinning column, air in the middle of the column rises. The result is that the spinning column of air rotates in a vertical direction and drops below the thunderstorm to form a funnel cloud. When the funnel cloud touches the ground, it becomes a tornado.

A tornado can last anywhere from a few seconds to more than an hour. Most tornadoes last less than ten minutes. More than 1,000 tornadoes occur in the United States each year, but they are not evenly distributed across the country. Most tornadoes occur in the middle of continents. In the United States, the area where most tornadoes happen is called "Tornado Alley." You can find out about the average number of tornadoes per year in each state by studying the map.

EVIDENCE NOTEBOOK

13. As you explore this section, think about whether a tornado could suddenly bury a city and its inhabitants. Record your evidence.

Average Annual Number of Tornadoes in the United States, 1991–2010

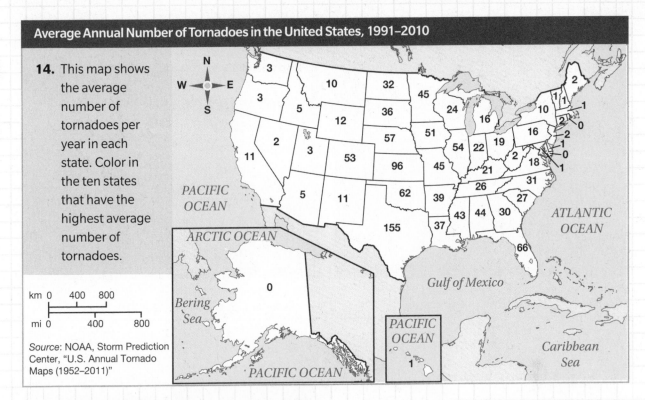

14. This map shows the average number of tornadoes per year in each state. Color in the ten states that have the highest average number of tornadoes.

km 0 400 800

mi 0 400 800

Source: NOAA, Storm Prediction Center, "U.S. Annual Tornado Maps (1952–2011)"

Tornado Classification and Hazards

When a tornado strikes a populated area and is strong enough, it can cause damage, injury, or death. Its strong winds destroy many objects in its path, including buildings, roads, trees, crops, and sometimes people and other animals. A tornado that causes these types of damage is considered a natural disaster.

Meteorologists collect tornado data, such as a tornado's path, wind speeds, duration, and temperatures. These data are organized into tables, graphs, and maps and then analyzed to help us understand the causes of tornadoes and their effects on people and the environment. Tornado data are also analyzed to identify areas at risk for tornado hazards and to make predictions about when and where tornadoes might occur. The Enhanced Fujita (foo•JEE•tuh) Scale, also known as the EF Scale, describes tornado damage.

The Enhanced Fujita Scale		
EF rating	**Wind speeds (km/h)**	**Expected damage**
EF-0	105–137	Chimneys damaged; tree branches broken; shallow-rooted trees toppled.
EF-1	138–177	Roof surfaces peeled off; windows broken; some tree trunks snapped; garages may be destroyed.
EF-2	178–217	Roofs damaged; manufactured homes destroyed; trees snapped or uprooted; debris entered air.
EF-3	218–266	Roofs and walls torn from buildings; some small buildings destroyed; most forest trees uprooted.
EF-4	267–322	Well-built homes destroyed; cars lifted and blown some distance; large debris flew through the air.
EF-5	Over 323	Strong houses lifted, concrete structures damaged; very large debris flew through the air; trees debarked.

Source: NOAA

15. These photos show different places where a tornado occurred. How would you rate the damage caused by each tornado based on the Enhanced Fujita (EF) Scale?

This tornado uprooted a few shallow-rooted trees and damaged many chimneys in the neighborhood.

This tornado damaged all of the homes in this community and tossed large debris and several cars through the air.

Language SmArts
Compare Tornado Data

16. A researcher wants to collect tornado data from the three states where tornado risk is highest. Where and when should the researcher collect data? Support your claim by citing evidence from this graph and from the map of tornadoes in the United States.

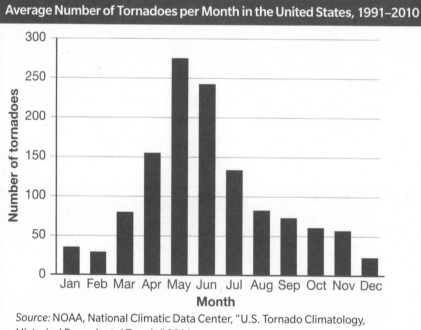

Average Number of Tornadoes per Month in the United States, 1991–2010

Source: NOAA, National Climatic Data Center, "U.S. Tornado Climatology, Historical Records and Trends," 2011

Continue Your Exploration

Name: _____   Date: _____

Check out the path below or go online to choose one of the other paths shown.

| The Cost of Natural Disasters | • **People in Science** • **Forest Fires** • **Hands-On Labs** 🖐 • **Propose Your Own Path** | *Go online to choose one of these other paths.* |

Natural disasters can destroy homes, buildings, crops, and sources of clean water. They can also cause injury and death. It can be very costly to repair the damage caused by a natural disaster. The cost can be determined by considering many factors, such as

- What was damaged or destroyed?
- Do the inhabitants of the area need to have those objects or systems repaired or replaced?
- What can be repaired and what must be replaced?
- What materials and labor are needed to repair or replace objects or systems?

Once the necessary work is identified, someone will have to pay for it. The costs are paid by insurance companies; local, state, and federal agencies; government disaster relief programs; nonprofit organizations, and the individuals who live in the area.

Natural Disasters in the United States

In 2015, one of the most expensive types of natural disaster in the United States was the tropical cyclone. *Tropical cyclone* is a term used by scientists to refer to any rotating, organized storm that starts over tropical waters. Environmental changes resulting from rising temperatures have increased the frequency and intensity of tropical cyclones.

These storms cause massive and widespread destruction by bringing high winds, heavy rains, and possible tornadoes and flooding to large areas. The wind and flooding from *tropical cyclones* can affect people in populated areas by damaging buildings, roads, dams, sea walls, and other structures along coastlines and waterways.

These men are pushing a vehicle off a flooded road in Houston, Texas, after heavy rains fell during Hurricane Harvey.

Continue Your Exploration

Billion-Dollar Weather and Climate Disasters in the United States, 1980–2016		
Disaster type	**Number of events**	**Cost of damage (in billions of dollars)**
Tropical cyclone	35	560.1
Drought/heat wave	24	223.8
Severe local storm	83	180.1
Nontropical flood	26	110.7
Winter storm	14	41.3
Wildfire	14	33.0
Freeze	7	25.3

Source: NOAA National Centers for Environmental Information (NCEI), U.S. Billion-Dollar Weather and Climate Disasters, January 2017

1. **Do the Math** Compare the cost of damage caused by tropical cyclones and by severe local storms, and compare the number of each of those events. Was the average cost of damage per event higher for tropical cyclones or for severe local storms?

2. How could you explain this difference?

3. Which costs would be associated with a severe freeze in an apple orchard? Select all that apply.

    A. recovering from the cost of a loss of apples

    B. replacing damaged or destroyed trees

    C. repairing irrigation lines that burst when they froze

    D. buying new harvesting equipment

. With a partner, discuss ways that encouraging volunteers to participate
efforts could reduce the time for recovering from a natural hazard.

Can You Explain It?

Name: _____   Date: _____

How was this city suddenly buried without warning?

EVIDENCE NOTEBOOK

Refer to the notes in your Evidence Notebook to help you construct an explanation for what could have suddenly buried this city.

1. State your claim. Make sure your claim fully explains what could have suddenly buried this city and its people, and why the people were unable to escape.

2. Summarize the evidence you have gathered to support your claim and explain your reasoning.

Checkpoints

Answer the following questions to check your understanding of the lesson.

3. A volcanic eruption produces a pyroclastic flow, a dense cloud of hot ash. How might the pyroclastic flow disrupt the local ecosystem? Select all that apply.

   A. by partially blocking the sunlight to the area

   B. by contaminating water supplies in the area

   C. by killing all of the vegetation in its path

   D. by damaging roads and buildings in its path

Use the photo to answer Question 4.

4. Which of the following natural hazards could have caused the ash damage in this photo? Select all that apply.

   A. flood

   B. hurricane

   C. volcanic eruption

   D. earthquake

   E. wildfire

Use the graph to answer Questions 5–6.

5. Which of the following statements is true?

   A. The number of tornadoes per year remains about the same.

   B. The number of tornadoes per year varies from year to year.

   C. The number of tornadoes per year is increasing each year.

   D. The number of tornadoes per year is decreasing each year.

   ...ich of the following periods ...west tornadoes?

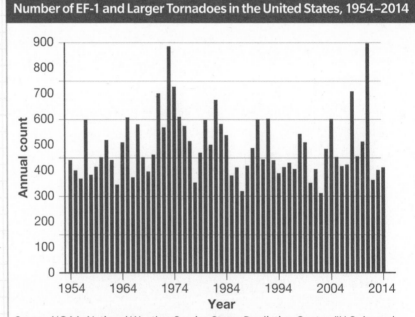

Number of EF-1 and Larger Tornadoes in the United States, 1954–2014

Source: NOAA, National Weather Service Storm Prediction Center, "U.S. Annual Count of EF-1+ Tornadoes, 1954 through 2014"

Interactive Review

Complete this section to review the main concepts of the lesson.

Natural hazards are naturally occurring events such as wildfires, earthquakes, and hurricanes. Natural disasters are natural hazards that negatively affect humans.

A. Provide two examples of natural hazards that are not natural disasters.

A volcanic eruption is a geologic hazard. Any type of volcanic eruption can become a natural disaster.

B. Describe a volcanic hazard and explain how it could become a natural disaster.

A tornado is a weather hazard that forms quickly and with little warning. A tornado can become a natural disaster.

C. Describe how the terms "Tornado Alley" and "tornado season" are related to the analysis of data about tornadoes.

Some Natural Hazards Can Be Predicted and Mitigated

This flood in New Jersey was caused by the melting of snow and ice after a major snowstorm. Understanding weather patterns can help people forecast natural hazards like floods.

Explore First

Modeling a Flood What patterns can help us predict when and where a flood might occur? Design a landscape using modeling clay inside a small waterproof container. Use a spray bottle filled with water to model rainfall or pour water slowly from a cup to model a river overflowing its banks. What do you observe as more water is added?

Go online to view the digital version of the Hands-On Lab for this lesson and to download additional lab resources.

CAN YOU EXPLAIN IT?

Why is there a tsunami hazard warning sign on this calm beach?

This beach on the east coast of New Zealand is a popular recreation spot.

1. Some coastal areas are at a higher risk for tsunamis than others are. How do we know which coastal areas are more likely to be affected by tsunamis?

 EVIDENCE NOTEBOOK As you explore this lesson, gather evidence to help explain how we know which coastal areas are at risk for tsunamis.

Predicting Natural Hazards

If the sky is full of dark clouds, you might predict that rain is about to fall. Making predictions is an important part of science. Natural hazard predictions can minimize damage from natural disasters because warnings can be issued to help people prepare.

2. People living near this stream think that if heavy rains continue, the stream will overflow and flood their homes. What information might these people be using to make this prediction?

When it rains, water runs downhill and collects along the lowest elevations in an area, such as this stream.

Natural Hazard Predictions

Natural hazard predictions are efforts to forecast the occurrence, intensity, and effects of natural hazards. Some natural hazards are not predictable. Other hazards follow known patterns, or are preceded by precursor events. If precursor events, or patterns, can be detected far enough in advance, a prediction may be made. For example, a precursor event to a flood may be heavy rainfall over a short period of time. Natural hazard predictions can help people reduce the effects of a natural hazard or even prevent some natural disasters.

Natural hazard predictions involve some uncertainty. Uncertainties can include a hazard's exact location, timing, magnitude, and whether it will actually happen. Certainty generally increases as the time of the predicted event gets closer. Natural hazard predictions are improved by gaining a scientific understanding of hazards, collecting and analyzing data, and using monitoring technology. Advances in science and technology can help improve natural hazard predictions. These advances can help us prepare for the effects of natural hazards. Societal needs, such as keeping people safe, drive development of these advances.

Scientific Understanding

A natural hazard prediction can be improved by gaining scientific understanding of a natural hazard. To gain scientific understanding, you can start by asking questions that can be answered by using scientific methods. For example, if you wanted to understand more about avalanches, you might ask: On which slopes are avalanches most common? What weather conditions are related to avalanches? What types of snow are related to avalanches? To answer these kinds of questions, you can collect and analyze data, use models, or conduct experiments. These practices help scientists better understand natural hazards.

Scientists analyze the snow conditions on slopes to determine how likely an avalanche is to occur.

Historical Data

Historical data are used to evaluate the likelihood that a natural hazard will happen in a given place. Historical data can include the locations of past events, as well as their frequency, magnitude, and effects on the environment and/or people. Some hazards, such as volcanic eruptions, landslides, and earthquakes, tend to occur in specific areas. However, these hazards can happen at any time of the year. Hazards, such as hurricanes and tornadoes, tend to happen in specific places and during specific times of the year.

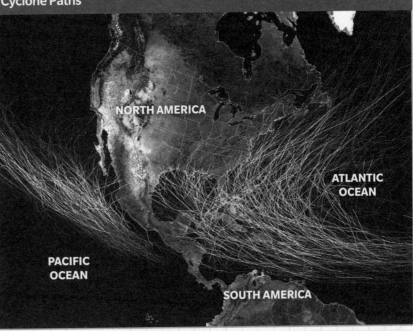

Historical Hurricane and Tropical Cyclone Paths

The lines on this map show the paths of past hurricanes and tropical cyclones. These data help us identify where hurricanes are likely to occur in the future.

Hurricane Paths

—— Hurricane

—— Tropical cyclone (intensity below major hurricane)

Atlantic Ocean data: 1851–2013
Pacific Ocean data: 1949–2013

Source: NOAA, Major Hurricane History of the U.S., 2013

NORTH AMERICA

ATLANTIC OCEAN

PACIFIC OCEAN

SOUTH AMERICA

Data from Monitoring

Scientists use technology to monitor conditions that relate to the occurrence of natural hazards. For example, satellites orbit Earth and collect weather data. These data go into computer models that help scientists predict weather-related hazards. For hazards that are likely to occur in specific locations, monitoring technology may be designed for and placed in those areas. For example, underwater earthquakes, landslides, and volcanic eruptions can be precursor events to tsunamis. So, scientists monitor ocean water movement after those events in order to predict tsunamis. Tsunami sensors might be put on buoys or on the sea floor to detect water movement in areas at high risk of tsunamis.

This tsunami in Miyako City, Japan, was caused by an earthquake on the ocean floor. The waves arrived less than one hour after the earthquake. Luckily, many people received warnings before the waves struck thanks to monitoring data.

EVIDENCE NOTEBOOK

3. How might scientific understanding, historical data, and monitoring help to determine where tsunami hazard signs should be placed? Record your evidence.

Atmospheric Administration (NOAA)

Hands-On Lab
Predict a Landslide

You will model the relationship between rainfall, hill slope, and landslides.

Heavy rain is forecast for Pineville. Historical data for this area show that heavy rains increase the chance of landslides. Landslides occur when soil and rock slide down a slope and can travel fast and threaten lives and property.

Procedure

STEP 1 Look at the slopes on the map and the slope angles in the table. On which slopes do you predict landslides are likely to occur?

STEP 2 One at a time, model Slopes 1, 2, 3, and 4. Place the chute so one end is at the edge of the plastic tub and tape it to the inside wall of the tub. The other end of the chute should be inside the tub.

STEP 3 To model Slope 1, rest the chute on the edge of the tub. Use the scoop to fill the top $\frac{1}{3}$ of the chute with damp soil.

STEP 4 Outside of the tub and under the chute, set up the protractor to measure the angle between the table and the bottom edge of the chute. Have a partner slowly tilt the chute until the angle is about 10 degrees.

STEP 5 Spray the slope to simulate rainfall until the soil is saturated. Record your observations in the table.

STEP 6 Model Slopes 2, 3, and 4 by repeating STEPS 3–5. Why should you use the same amount of soil and spray the water in a consistent way for all of the trials?

MATERIALS
• duct tape
• gutter, vinyl, U-shaped, 60 cm section (chute)
• plastic scoop
• plastic tub, shallow
• potting soil, saturated
• protractor
• spray bottle

Landslide Model Data

Slope angle (degrees)	Results
Slope 1: 10°	
Slope 2: 15°	
Slope 3: 35°	
Slope 4: 55°	

Landslide Study Area for Pineville

This map shows how the Pineville area is surrounded by hillsides. The hillsides are generally made up of the same type of soil and have little vegetation. Rainfall amounts are even across the area.

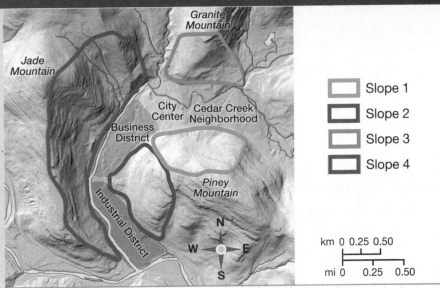

Slope 1
Slope 2
Slope 3
Slope 4

Analysis

STEP 7 Soil on steeper slopes requires *less / more* rain to result in a landslide than the soil on flatter slopes does.

STEP 8 Compare your prediction to your results. Was your prediction correct?

STEP 9 Based on your model, are any areas in Pineville at risk of damage from a landslide? Explain why or why not.

STEP 10 Evaluate your model. What did your model represent well? What could be changed or added to improve your model?

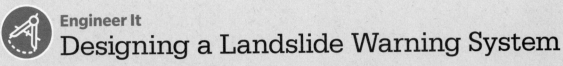

Engineer It
Designing a Landslide Warning System

4. What information is needed in order to design a landslide warning system that can save lives in Pineville? How would you warn the residents of Pineville that a landslide is likely to occur?

_____

_____

_____

_____

_____

Predicting Geologic Hazards

Geologic hazards include volcanoes, earthquakes, tsunamis, sinkholes, and landslides. Different areas experience different geologic hazards. For example, areas near tectonic plate boundaries experience more earthquakes than areas far from plate boundaries do. The likelihood of a geologic hazard occurring in a specific location can be determined. But the timing and magnitude of geologic hazards are difficult to predict.

Worldwide Distribution of Earthquakes and Volcanoes

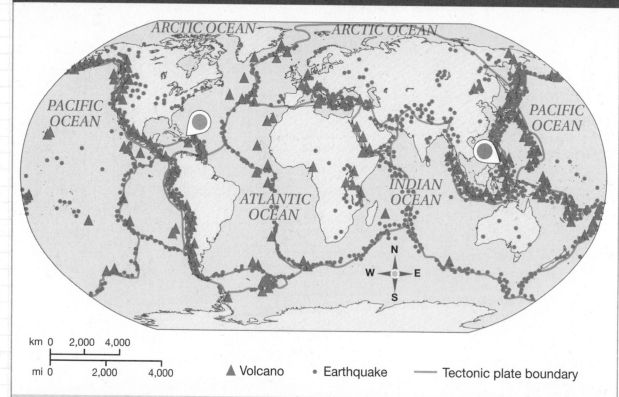

▲ Volcano   • Earthquake   —— Tectonic plate boundary

In 2010, a major earthquake shook the ground and toppled buildings in Haiti. Earthquakes happen suddenly and currently cannot be predicted.

Scientists predicted the eruption of Mount Pinatubo in 1991. The predictions helped thousands of people evacuate before falling ash and lahars destroyed villages.

5. **Discuss** Look at the photo of the effects of the Mount Pinatubo eruption. Predicting volcanic eruptions, such as this one, can save lives and prevent injuries. How do you think scientists predicted this eruption?

Predictions of Volcanic Eruptions

Predictions of volcanic eruptions usually include the likelihood of an eruption within a given time frame. They might also identify possible hazardous effects or related hazards, such as lava flows or wildfires. To determine the likelihood of a volcanic eruption, scientists analyze data, such as the locations of active volcanoes or a certain volcano's past eruptions. Eruption predictions are not always certain because most volcanoes do not erupt on regular schedules. Before some eruptions, specific conditions or precursor events can be identified. Therefore, scientists monitor some volcanoes to watch for changes in conditions and precursor events. Data from monitoring help scientists predict the likelihood of an eruption. However, precursor events and changes in a volcano's conditions may occur without ending in an eruption.

Scientific Understanding

Scientists study the causes and effects of volcanic eruptions. Scientists know that before an eruption, molten rock in Earth's interior, called *magma*, moves closer to the surface. The movement of the magma cracks the surrounding rock and causes swarms of small earthquakes. The moving magma also releases gases into the air and causes the ground surface to change shape.

Scientists study volcanoes to determine whether a volcano is active. They also see whether an eruption could result in a natural disaster. Because scientists have identified where active volcanoes exist around the world, they can identify areas that are at risk for eruption-related natural disasters. For example, the map shows that there are many active volcanoes along the west coasts of North and South America.

This lava flowed over 20 km downhill from the Kilauea volcano. It stopped just outside the town of Pahoa, Hawaii.

Data from Past Eruptions

Past eruption data for a volcano can include eruption timing, precursor events, and eruption types. For example, volcanic rocks and ash layers from past eruptions can tell how often and how explosively a volcano has erupted in the past. This helps scientists determine whether a volcano is active and what type of eruption, if any, is likely to happen in the future. For example, a volcano that explosively erupted and made large amounts of ash in the past most likely will have a similar eruption in the future.

Mauna Loa is an active volcano located on the Big Island of Hawaii. It is a *shield volcano*. This means that it is a broad dome with gently sloping sides. Shield volcanoes often have steady lava flows rather than explosive eruptions. Many eruptions of Mauna Loa have been witnessed by people living in Hawaii. For safety, scientists monitor many active volcanoes near populated areas.

Mauna Loa Eruption Data ,1832–2004	
General Information	**Eruption History**
Location: Mauna Loa, Hawaii	1832, 1843, 1849, 1851, 1852, 1855–1856, 1859, 1865–1866, 1870 (?)*, 1871, 1872, 1873, 1873–1874, 1875, 1876, 1877, 1879, 1880, 1880–1881, 1887, 1892, 1896, 1899, 1903, 1907, 1914–1915, 1916, 1919, 1926, 1933, 1935–1936, 1940, 1950, 1975, 1984
Type and Elevation: Shield volcano, 4,170 m (13,681 ft)	
Eruption Style: Nonexplosive, with steady lava flows	

*The question mark indicates that the exact year of the eruption is not known.
Source: USGS, Hawaii Volcano Observatory, "Summary of Historical Eruptions, 1843–Present", 2004

6. Mauna Loa erupted on average once every four years between 1832 and 1984. From 1870 to 1880, the number of eruptions was *greater / fewer* than average. Beginning in 1940, eruptions were *more / less* frequent than average.

Monitoring Volcanoes

Scientists monitor volcanoes by using technology that detects slight changes in the ground and air around a volcano. They use GPS instruments and thermal imaging sensors set on planes and satellites. These instruments show if magma is moving or if the ground is changing shape. They use *seismometers,* which detect vibrations in the ground, to monitor earthquake activity. Increases in local earthquakes can show movements of magma before a volcanic eruption. Scientists also use *tiltmeters* to monitor changes in the volcano's shape that are related to pressure changes inside the volcano. They also measure the concentration of gases around volcanic vents because the volcano may release more of these gases just before an eruption.

Scientists use tiltmeters to see if a volcano is expanding or shrinking. They use GPS stations to see how much the surface of a volcano is moving.

Change in Distance Across Mauna Loa's Summit Crater, 2010–2015

GPS units measure the change in distance between Stations 1 and 2.

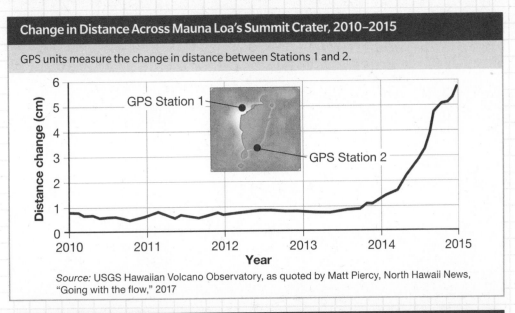

Source: USGS Hawaiian Volcano Observatory, as quoted by Matt Piercy, North Hawaii News, "Going with the flow," 2017

Mauna Loa's Earthquake Activity, 2010–2015

This graph shows the frequency of earthquakes on Mauna Loa.

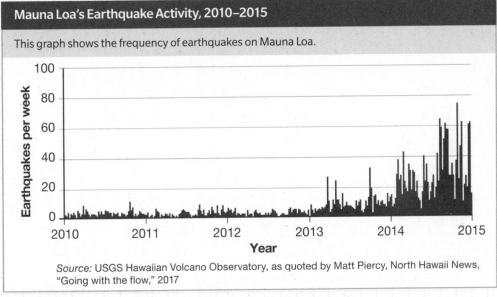

Source: USGS Hawaiian Volcano Observatory, as quoted by Matt Piercy, North Hawaii News, "Going with the flow," 2017

7. The graphs show that Mauna Loa's crater *expanded / shrank* and the number of earthquakes *increased / decreased*.

Earthquake Prediction

Earthquakes can become natural disasters because the shaking can damage structures. Earthquakes can also cause tsunamis, fires, and landslides. Scientists are able to identify areas where earthquakes are likely to happen and cause damage. Scientists use historical data, seismograph data, and GPS data to make earthquake risk maps. These maps show the relative likelihood of an earthquake of a specific size happening in a given area within a given time frame.

EVIDENCE NOTEBOOK

8. What kinds of data might scientists collect in order to identify where tsunamis are likely to occur? How can scientists predict when tsunamis are likely to occur? Record your evidence.

Probability of a Magnitude 7.0 Earthquake near Yellowstone National Park

A magnitude 7.0 earthquake is a large earthquake that could cause major damage, injury, or death.

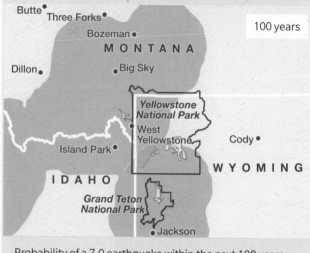

100 years

Probability of a 7.0 earthquake within the next 100 years.

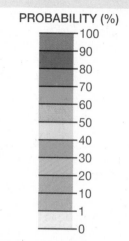

PROBABILITY (%)

— 100
— 90
— 80
— 70
— 60
— 50
— 40
— 30
— 20
— 10
— 1
— 0

Source: USGS, Geologic Hazards Science Center, National Seismic Hazard Mapping Project, 2009

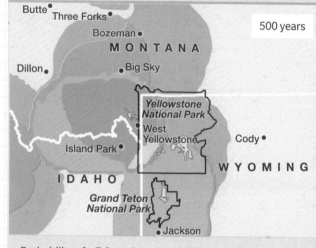

500 years

Probability of a 7.0 earthquake within the next 500 years.

1,000 years

Probability of a 7.0 earthquake within the next 1,000 years.

9. The probability of a magnitude 7.0 earthquake happening in Bozeman, Montana, in the next 100 years is 0–1% / 1–10% / 10–20%.

Do the Math
Explain Earthquake Probability

10. Choose Big Sky, Island Park, or Jackson. Use the key to explain how the chance of a magnitude 7.0 earthquake relates to the length of time for which the projection is made for the town you have chosen.

_____

_____

_____

_____

Predicting Weather and Climate Hazards

Weather hazards include thunderstorms, snowstorms, tornadoes, and floods. These hazards occur in locations where the atmosphere, ocean, and land interact to create specific conditions. Weather predictions describe what the weather is likely to be on a particular day. A weather-hazard prediction indicates when and where dangerous weather conditions are likely to develop. Warnings about weather hazards are issued only minutes to days before a potential event.

    Climate hazards are large-scale phenomena that are related to long-term weather patterns. Climate hazards include droughts, sea-level changes, and wildfires.

Worldwide Tornado Risk

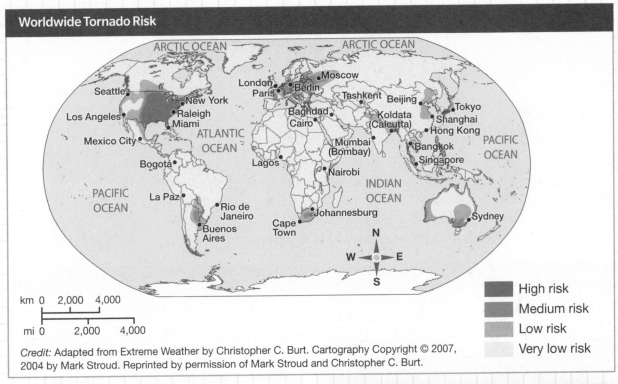

High risk
Medium risk
Low risk
Very low risk

Credit: Adapted from Extreme Weather by Christopher C. Burt. Cartography Copyright © 2007, 2004 by Mark Stroud. Reprinted by permission of Mark Stroud and Christopher C. Burt.

11. Look at the map and the photo. We know where tornado risk is high, but do you think we can prevent tornadoes from causing damage and injury? Explain.

In 2011, a tornado destroyed this house in North Carolina. A tornado warning was issued about 24 minutes before the tornado struck the area.

12. Look at the map. What is California's tornado risk?

Predicting Weather Hazards

Predicting weather and climate hazards relies on understanding the complex ways that the atmosphere, oceans, and topography interact to create weather systems. Some types of weather hazards are related to each other, so scientists use an understanding of those patterns to forecast and predict weather and climate events with varying certainty. Agencies such as the National Oceanic and Atmospheric Administration (NOAA) and the National Weather Service (NWS) continually gather and monitor weather data using technology. For example, although scientists have a pretty good understanding of the conditions that lead to tornadoes, they are difficult to predict with any certainty.

Scientific Understanding

Meteorologists know a lot about conditions that are likely to cause thunderstorms, hurricanes, and even tornadoes. They understand the movement of air masses of different temperatures and moisture content, and that knowledge helps them predict when different weather conditions may occur. Some weather conditions are seasonal, some are cyclical, and many can be predicted within a certain range of probability and within a certain amount of time. For example, the El Niňo–Southern Oscillation (ENSO) is a climate pattern that affects the Pacific Ocean in cycles of one to seven years. This system has an effect on global climate patterns.

Historical Data

Meteorologists analyze historical data to determine when and where tornadoes are most common. In the United States, tornadoes tend to strike during late afternoons and evenings during spring, summer, and fall. However, tornadoes have struck in the morning and in winter. Scientists also analyze historical data, such as this map of tornado tracks in the United States, to determine where tornadoes are most common.

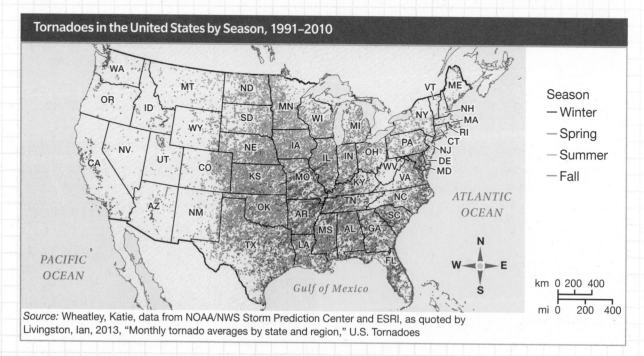

Tornadoes in the United States by Season, 1991–2010

Season
— Winter
— Spring
— Summer
— Fall

Source: Wheatley, Katie, data from NOAA/NWS Storm Prediction Center and ESRI, as quoted by Livingston, Ian, 2013, "Monthly tornado averages by state and region," U.S. Tornadoes

13. The tornado data on this map show a pattern. In the northernmost states where tornadoes occur, most tornadoes occur in the
winter / spring / summer / fall. In the southeastern United States, most tornadoes occur in the winter / spring / summer / fall.

Forecasting Tornadoes

Meteorologists look at wind patterns in supercell thunderstorms that show rotation. Tornadoes can form where the rotation is strong enough. This table and map were made from weather monitoring data. The data were gathered before and during a tornado outbreak in Raleigh, North Carolina, and the surrounding region in 2011.

Weather Forecasts for Raleigh, NC, from April 12 to April 16, 2011	
April 12, 2011	Forecast mentions a likely threat of upcoming severe weather on the evening of April 15th.
April 13, 2011	Forecast of severe weather is shifted to the daytime of April 16th.
April 14, 2011	NWS issues a prediction of a 30% chance of a major severe weather event on the 16th.
April 15, 2011	The likelihood of a severe weather event is increased to 45% and tornadoes are deemed "likely" to occur.
April 16, 2011	In the morning, NWS issues a warning for afternoon severe thunderstorms and tornadoes. In the afternoon, more than 30 tornadoes strike. Tornado warnings are issued for specific areas an average of 20–30 minutes before the tornadoes strike.

Source: National Weather Service, Raleigh, NC, "April 16, 2011, North Carolina Tornado Outbreak Event Summary," 2012

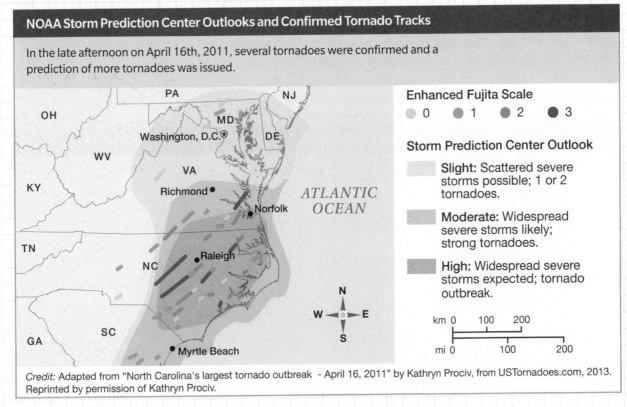

NOAA Storm Prediction Center Outlooks and Confirmed Tornado Tracks

In the late afternoon on April 16th, 2011, several tornadoes were confirmed and a prediction of more tornadoes was issued.

Enhanced Fujita Scale
0   1   2   3

Storm Prediction Center Outlook

Slight: Scattered severe storms possible; 1 or 2 tornadoes.

Moderate: Widespread severe storms likely; strong tornadoes.

High: Widespread severe storms expected; tornado outbreak.

Credit: Adapted from "North Carolina's largest tornado outbreak - April 16, 2011" by Kathryn Prociv, from USTornadoes.com, 2013. Reprinted by permission of Kathryn Prociv.

14. How did the information available in the weather forecasts change in the days leading up to April 16th? Do you think these forecasts gave people enough time to prepare for the tornadoes? Explain.

Monitoring

Several types of technologies are used to monitor weather conditions. For example, Doppler radar uses radio waves to identify direction and intensity of precipitation, wind direction and speed, and the locations of boundaries between large air masses. Weather satellites collect data on cloud systems, snow fields, and ocean currents. Weather stations record temperatures, precipitation, humidity, and wind speed. Historical records are kept and used to determine climate characteristics for a region and to recognize longer-term cycles or patterns.

Weather satellites are sometimes launched from Vandenberg Air Force base in California.

Predicting Floods

Flooding happens when land that is normally dry is covered by water. There are three main types of floods: flash floods, overbank floods, and coastal floods. Flash floods occur suddenly as very fast moving water from excessive rainfall runs over land. Overbank floods happen slowly when rain or melting snow makes river or lake levels rise. Coastal floods happen when high winds or storms push ocean water onto shore.

To predict floods, scientists monitor amounts of rainfall and snow melt, as well as water levels in lakes, streams, and oceans. Scientists also consider how much water the ground can absorb and how water flow is affected by an area's landforms.

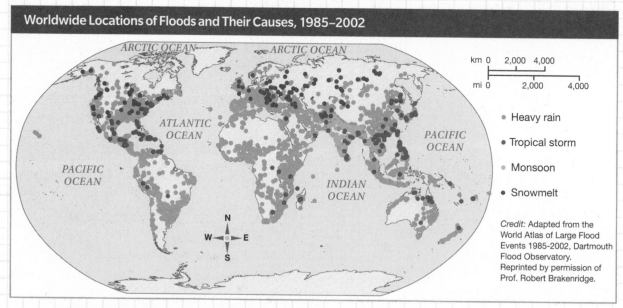

Worldwide Locations of Floods and Their Causes, 1985–2002

- Heavy rain
- Tropical storm
- Monsoon
- Snowmelt

Credit: Adapted from the World Atlas of Large Flood Events 1985-2002, Dartmouth Flood Observatory. Reprinted by permission of Prof. Robert Brakenridge.

15. The most widespread cause of flooding in the world is

heavy rain / tropical storms / monsoons / snowmelt.

Flooding caused by snowmelt mainly affected the

Northern / Southern hemisphere.

The region most affected by monsoonal rains is

North America / South America / Europe / Africa / Asia.

Language SmArts
Use Flood Maps

Historical data are used to create flood-risk maps to show how likely areas are to flood under certain conditions. When locations that can flood are identified, the effect of the floods on people can be predicted. It is important that people know safe routes to get out of flood-prone areas. Evacuation routes connect evacuation zones, or areas to be evacuated, to evacuation centers, where people can go to be safe during a flood event.

Flood Risk in New York City

This flood-risk map of New York City shows the evacuation zones for the areas that flood.

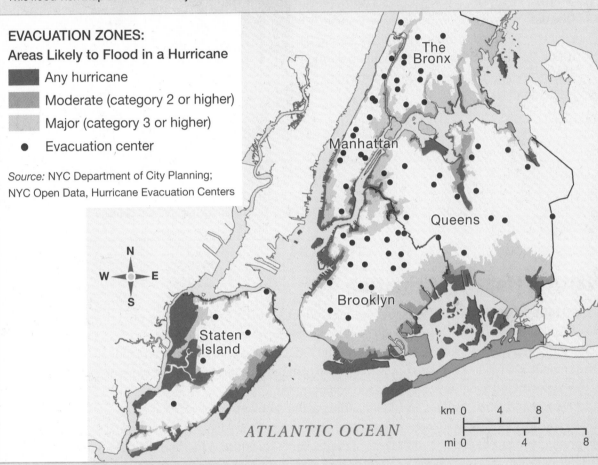

EVACUATION ZONES:
Areas Likely to Flood in a Hurricane
- Any hurricane
- Moderate (category 2 or higher)
- Major (category 3 or higher)
- Evacuation center

Source: NYC Department of City Planning; NYC Open Data, Hurricane Evacuation Centers

16. A moderate hurricane in the Atlantic Ocean is heading toward New York City. Based on the map, identify the areas that have a high chance of flooding during and after this storm. Suggest which areas people should evacuate based on the coming storm, and support your claim with evidence and reasoning.

_____

_____

_____

_____

_____

_____

Describing Natural Hazard Mitigation

Natural hazards such as floods, earthquakes, and severe storms are dangerous events. These events may cause harm to people and property and, sometimes, they happen without warning. Scientists, engineers, and community officials work together to prepare for and minimize the damage caused by natural hazards.

17. Discuss With a partner, discuss how a house could be designed to protect it from the strong winds, flooding, and erosion that happen during a hurricane. Record the key points from your discussion.

We cannot stop hurricanes, but we can build houses, like this one, that minimize the potential damage caused by this type of hazard.

Natural Hazard Mitigation

Hazard **mitigation** describes efforts to prevent or reduce property damage or loss of life caused by a natural disaster. Although people cannot prevent natural disasters, a good mitigation plan can help keep people safe and reduce damage to property and the environment when a disaster does occur. Mitigation plans are specific to different types of natural hazards and to different locations and communities.

Hazard mitigation requires an understanding of the problems involved. Scientists collect and analyze data about natural hazards and disasters. These data help scientists understand the causes and possible effects of these events. Scientists also use these data to determine if an area is at risk for a natural hazard. Scientists work with engineers to apply what they have learned from the data. They design solutions and develop ways to predict and, if possible, to control the hazard or its effects. Engineers and planners use data to develop mitigation strategies. Different strategies are used before, during, and after a natural hazard. Before the event, engineers focus on preparation. After a disaster, their focus shifts to a response to the disaster and recovery from its effects.

18. What types of data might be useful in mitigation efforts for an area that experiences frequent floods? Choose all that apply.

   A. historical information on rainfall patterns

   B. elevation mapping of the area

   C. average income of residents of the area

   D. location of population centers in the region

Preparation

Preparation is an important mitigation strategy. People prepare for disasters at many different levels. For example, mitigation planning is performed by individuals, families, communities, and local or federal governments.

Governments and other agencies develop and test plans in advance for how to respond to and recover from disastrous events. They work with scientists and engineers to develop technologies to monitor conditions, to make predictions, and to communicate with the public. They monitor conditions and share information before, during, and after natural hazards. Emergency management agencies find good locations for shelters and collect supplies to help people affected by a disaster.

Governments and communities can prepare by setting standards, also called *building codes.* These codes require structures to be likely to survive hazardous events and to protect people during these events. Architects and engineers design and build structures to meet these standards using different materials based on their properties.

Preparation includes education, so that people know what to expect, what to do, and where to go. If you know what hazards exist in your area and pay attention to predictions, you can prepare for the effects of natural hazards. Then, when you need to act, you will know what to do and you will have the things that you need in order to face the emergency.

If you are prepared, you are less likely to be severely affected by an event. If you learn what to expect during and after a natural hazard, you can identify what supplies you will need in case a disaster occurs. You can build an emergency kit as part of your preparations. Many kits include flashlights and batteries, blankets, first-aid supplies, fresh water, and other necessary items.

Being prepared helps people avoid some of the harmful effects of natural hazards. It also helps them recover after an event.

Scientists monitor conditions that lead to volcanic mudflows, called *lahars*, at Mount St. Helens. They use the data to predict lahars and warn people before a disaster occurs.

Television, radio, and emergency websites communicate information about weather hazards before, during, and after an event, such as a hurricane.

Preparation includes actions to prevent disasters. Restored wetlands help control water flow and reduce flooding.

19. A mitigation plan may define how people can be notified about the time and location of potential hazards. Weather forecasts provide information that communities need to *prepare for / respond to* natural hazards such as severe storms. During the emergency, governments and residents must be ready to *prepare for / respond to* changing local conditions.

Response

Natural hazard mitigation continues after the event begins. Appropriate and timely response helps reduce the negative effects of the hazard. Governments, relief agencies, and individuals can all respond to natural hazards. Responding to a natural hazard event means providing people with information and services as an event occurs and later. For example, during a flood, some responders rescue people whose homes or cars are surrounded by water. Others provide first aid and transportation to people who are injured or stranded.

Technology plays an important role in disaster response. Some technologies are used to monitor changing conditions. Other technologies, such as radios and phones, are essential for communication. Modern mapping technology helps responders reach affected locations as quickly as possible. Portable medical equipment and temporary shelters are used by doctors and nurses to provide care wherever or whenever it is needed.

Firefighters respond to a wildfire by using water and other chemicals to keep the fire from spreading.

Recovery

Emergency preparation and response efforts reduce damage and injury but they cannot prevent all damage or loss. Recovery is the final part of a mitigation plan. Recovery generally occurs after a disaster, but planning for recovery takes place long before it is needed. In some cases, recovery efforts may start before the event is over.

Recovering from a natural disaster may involve providing temporary shelter and services until permanent repairs can be made. Recovery involves providing supplies such as food, water, and medical supplies wherever they are needed as quickly as possible. Recovery also involves rebuilding and repairing damaged structures. The final step of recovery involves reviewing and revising mitigation plans for greater success in the future. Recovery is performed by government agencies, volunteer organizations, and members of a community.

Professionals and volunteers work together to help a community recover from a natural disaster.

EVIDENCE NOTEBOOK

20. Which phase of mitigation does a tsunami warning sign on a calm beach mainly support? Record your evidence.

21. These photos show three different parts of earthquake mitigation. Examine each photo and its caption. Then use the words from the word bank to label each photo with the stage of mitigation that is illustrated.

WORD BANK
- preparation
- recovery
- response

preparation

Students practice ways to protect themselves from falling objects during an earthquake.

Teams of volunteers and professionals search through rubble to rescue survivors of an earthquake.

Volunteers travel to areas affected by earthquakes to help residents rebuild homes and infrastructure.

22. Choose one of the examples from the photos. Suggest another mitigation activity that could be performed during that phase of hazard mitigation.

The Role of Technology in Mitigation Planning

Technology is important at all stages of natural hazard mitigation. It is useful in identifying hazard probability, in developing mitigation plans, in testing solutions, in response and recovery, and in evaluating the success of mitigation activities after a hazard. Sometimes, solutions involve developing new technologies, such as equipment or processes, or redesigning existing technologies. The uses of technologies are driven by the needs of the people in an area and the hazards they face. However, the availability of technology may be limited by location or by the economic conditions of a community or region.

One important technology used by scientists and engineers is computer modeling. Data gathered from monitoring stations, drones, and satellites are entered into programs that model and predict hazardous situations. A Geographic Information System (GIS) can then display maps and other visuals. Seeing trends in data over time is important when making decisions such as where to place levees along rivers to prevent flooding. Knowing when and where different kinds of natural hazard are most likely to occur helps reduce response and recovery times. Emergency shelters and medical relief can be sent where they will be needed more quickly.

Scientific Knowledge and Engineering Design Principles

Natural hazard mitigation relies on science and engineering for success. Scientists study the causes and effects of natural hazards. They apply what they learn to explain how, where, and why hazardous events may occur. This information is then used to mitigate the events' effects. For example, scientists study the conditions in the atmosphere that may lead to the formation of tornadoes. They use this information to decide which conditions to monitor in order to predict tornadoes. Scientists and engineers can then develop instruments such as satellites and radar systems to monitor the atmosphere. They design computer models to analyze the collected data. When the conditions are right for tornadoes to form, scientists issue warnings that tornadoes may happen.

Mitigation plans are developed by using the engineering design process. Scientists and engineers identify a problem that needs to be solved. Problems may include how to evacuate areas at risk of a disaster or how to get emergency supplies to people affected by a disaster. Once engineers identify a problem or need, they conduct research and more clearly define the problem. They then propose, evaluate, and test solutions to the problem. Solutions related to mitigating natural hazards could involve new tools or equipment. Other solutions could include new systems or processes.

Evaluate Mitigation Technologies

Tsunamis are giant waves that can be caused by an earthquake at the bottom of the ocean. Tsunami waves travel outward in all directions from the source. When the waves reach a shore, they can cause massive damage and loss of life. Scientists and engineers work to mitigate the hazards of tsunamis by developing ways to predict when one will occur and to issue timely warnings.

word bank
- saving lives
- preventing damage
- communication
- data collection
- environmental cleanup

23. Use the word bank to fill in the table to show which needs are met by the technologies that are shown. Some needs may be used more than once. Others may not be used at all.

	Technology	Meets Needs
	Scientists use seismographs to detect and record earthquakes. When an undersea earthquake occurs, scientists model the earthquake's effects to predict whether tsunamis may occur.	
	Evacuation plans are in place long before a tsunami occurs. Evacuation signs direct people to safe areas.	
	When data indicate that an earthquake has generated a tsunami, scientists use computers to determine where it is likely to strike. Then, scientists issue warnings to affected areas.	

Continue Your Exploration

Name: _____   Date: _____

Check out the path below or go online to choose one of the other paths shown.

Predicting Asteroid Impacts

- **Technology for Hurricane Forecasts**
- **Hands-On Labs** 🖐
- **Propose Your Own Path**

Go online to choose one of these other paths.

An *asteroid* is a large, rocky body that orbits the sun. Tens of thousands of asteroids orbit the sun between Mars and Jupiter. However, some asteroids pass close to Earth, and some even cross Earth's orbit. At times, small fragments of asteroids approach Earth, but most burn up as they travel through the atmosphere. People call these bright streaks of light "shooting stars." Scientists call them *meteors*. Some small fragments do not burn up entirely and they strike Earth, causing little to no damage. A larger asteroid impact could be a worldwide catastrophe, but this type of event is extremely rare. A large asteroid strikes Earth about once every 10,000 years.

Potentially Hazardous Asteroids

Scientists use monitoring technology, such as telescopes, to locate asteroids that orbit close to Earth. Automated systems are used to determine whether these asteroids could pose a threat to Earth. As monitoring technology continues to improve, new asteroids are continually identified. Some of these asteroids pass very close to Earth.

A *potentially hazardous asteroid* (PHA) is one that orbits close enough to Earth to pose a threat. A PHA must be large enough to survive the trip through the atmosphere and hit Earth's surface. Identified PHAs will not necessarily strike Earth's surface, but because an impact is possible, PHAs are continuously monitored. This ongoing monitoring helps scientists better predict whether a PHA poses a threat. The National Aeronautics and Space Administration (NASA) currently monitors more than 1,700 PHAs. As of 2018, no asteroids were categorized as an immediate threat to Earth in the near future.

The Barringer Crater in Arizona is the result of an asteroid impact about 50,000 years ago. The asteroid was about 50 meters wide.

Continue Your Exploration

1. Based on the table, how likely is a large asteroid impact in your lifetime? Explain.

Timeline of the Ten Biggest Known Asteroid Impacts on Earth	
Name of Crater	Time (millions of years ago)
Chesapeake Bay Crater, USA	35
Popigai Crater, Russia	36
Chicxulub Crater, Mexico	66
Kara Crater, Russia	70
Morokweng Crater, South Africa	145
Manicouagan Crater, Canada	214
Woodleigh Crater, Australia	364
Acraman Crater, Australia	580
Sudbury Crater, Canada	1,849
Vredefort Crater, South Africa	2,023

Source: National Geographic. "Asteroid Impacts: 10 Biggest Known Hits," 2013

2. Why are new PHAs continually discovered?

3. An asteroid over 100 meters in diameter could affect an entire country. Scientists predict that there is a 1% chance that an asteroid of this size could strike Earth in the next 100 years. What factors could cause the calculation of this probability to increase or decrease?

4. **Collaborate** Conduct research to evaluate the following statement: "The chances of a small asteroid affecting humans are greater than the chances of a large asteroid affecting humans." Cite evidence to support your evaluation.

Can You Explain It?

Name: **Date:**

Why is there a tsunami hazard warning sign on this calm beach?

TSUNAMI HAZARD ZONE

IN CASE OF A TSUNAMI ALERT GO TO HIGH GROUND OR ASSEMBLY AREA

Far North District Council

EVIDENCE NOTEBOOK

Refer to the notes in your Evidence Notebook to help you construct an explanation for how we know which coastal areas are at risk for tsunamis.

1.   State your claim. Make sure your claim fully explains why there is a tsunami hazard warning sign on a calm beach.

2.   Summarize the evidence you have gathered to support your claim and explain your reasoning.

Checkpoints

Answer the following questions to check your understanding of the lesson.

Use the photograph to answer Questions 3–5.

3. What information about the blizzard shown in the photo can be gathered that will help meteorologists make predictions about future blizzards? Select all that apply.

   A. the amount of snow that fell

   B. the location of the blizzard

   C. the amount of moisture in the air

   D. the temperature and wind direction

   E. the types of clouds present

4. A blizzard is a *geologic / weather* hazard that can be predicted using *satellite images / GPS data*. A hazard mitigation plan to reduce the *negative / positive* impacts of a blizzard might include sending text messages to warn people before the storm arrives.

5. Many cities do not allow parking on the street when a blizzard has been predicted. How might parked cars interfere with hazard mitigation?

   A. People cannot get the cars out of the parking spaces to drive to work.

   B. Parked cars force traffic to move slower.

   C. Snow-covered cars on the street slow down emergency responders.

   D. The cars make the snow appear worse than it actually is.

Use the table to answer Question 6.

Eruption History of Mt. Etna, Italy, 2002–2015										
2002	2003	2005	2006	2008	2009	2010	2011	2013	2014	2015

Source: Smithsonian Institution, Global Volcanism Program, Etna

6. Mt. Etna is an *active / extinct* volcano. Scientists should *occasionally / continuously* monitor changes in the shape of the volcano that may signal a volcanic eruption by using *seismometers / tiltmeters*.

7. How does a better scientific understanding of Earth's atmosphere and oceans help scientists predict natural hazards? Choose all that apply.

   A. Changes in the atmosphere and oceans trigger geologic hazards, such as earthquakes and volcanic eruptions.

   B. The atmosphere and oceans are primarily responsible for weather and climate patterns that could lead to hazards such as hurricanes or tornadoes.

   C. Understanding the atmosphere and oceans can help scientists develop new technologies to monitor conditions that could lead to hazardous events.

Interactive Review

Complete this page to review the main concepts of the lesson.

Scientists gather natural hazard data to improve scientific understanding, analyze historical occurrences, and monitor conditions to better predict natural hazards.

A. How can analyzing historical data and monitoring hazardous events help scientists improve their predictions of natural hazards?

Predicting geologic hazards requires understanding geologic processes, identifying precursor events, and monitoring sites where geologic hazards may occur.

B. Identify two geologic hazards that are related and explain their relationship.

Predicting weather and climate hazards requires understanding Earth system processes, identifying related historical events, and monitoring current weather conditions.

C. How do scientific understanding, historical data, and monitoring help scientists predict weather and climate hazards?

There are three parts to natural hazard mitigation: preparation, response, and recovery.

D. How does a hazard mitigation plan help a community deal with a disaster?

©Sarah D. Davis/

LESSON 4

Human Use of Synthetic Materials Affects Earth's Surface

This sea turtle is eating a plastic bottle. Plastic bags and other synthetic materials are often ingested by marine animals confusing these materials with real food.

Explore First

Exploring Synthetics Plastic objects often have a recycling symbol on them with a number from 1 to 7. These numbers are a code and can tell you if the object can be recycled. How many different recycling numbers can you find on plastic objects in your classroom?

Go online to view the digital version of
the Hands-On Lab for this lesson and to
download additional lab resources.

CAN YOU EXPLAIN IT?

How can engineers change the effects of the synthetic materials in the bottles on the environment by reusing the materials to make the jacket?

Plastic bottles and this polyester jacket are made of the same synthetic material.

1. Where have you seen plastic beverage bottles and polyester jackets?

2. What natural resource are the plastic bottles and polyester jacket made from?

EVIDENCE NOTEBOOK As you explore this lesson, gather evidence to explain how using the material from plastic bottles to make a jacket can reduce the environmental effects of the synthetic material on the environment.

Analyzing the Life Cycle of Synthetic Materials

You can find synthetic materials in your backpack, your closet, the refrigerator, and the medicine cabinet. Synthetic materials are materials that are made by humans using chemical processes. Synthetic materials are usually designed to have specific properties needed for a particular purpose. However, sometimes new materials are discovered by accident. For example, in the 1960s, Stephanie Kwolek was developing new polymers that could be used to make tires more durable. She discovered a new type of fiber that was extremely strong and lightweight. That fiber is Kevlar®. Its properties make it ideal for use in bulletproof vests and helmets. Engineers have designed different types of Kevlar® that have many uses. Some of the things Kevlar® is used in include vehicle armor, motorcycle racing gear, and tires.

Between the layers of black fabric in this bulletproof vest is a layer of protective synthetic material called *Kevlar*®.

3. How do the properties of Kevlar® determine how it is used?

Synthetic Materials and Society

Engineers look for ways to improve existing materials or design new materials as the needs of society change. New materials have made cars more lightweight, which means they burn less gasoline. New medicines are developed as scientists learn more about the causes of diseases. New materials help computers work faster.

4. Which of the following might drive the development of new materials? Select all that apply.

    A. a desire for affordable, fashionable clothing

    B. an idea that air pollution should be reduced

    C. a need for safe apartment buildings

    D. a change in the availability of natural resources

Needs

Synthetic materials are developed to meet the needs of people. Some needs are basic, such as food and water, energy, housing, and transportation. But even these needs have changed. Foods are now shipped all over the world and may be stored for long periods of time before they reach consumers. Synthetic materials that preserve food help it last longer. The population has increased and cities have grown. Synthetic building materials have made it possible to build larger buildings to house more people and businesses.

Desires

What things would you like to buy—trendy clothes, shoes of a famous basketball player, video games, or a bike like your friends have? People's desires also affect the types of materials that are developed and the way they are used. Materials may be developed to make products people want, such as running shoes or bicycle frames. Synthetic materials may also make products more affordable.

Values

Values affect the development and use of materials. Your values include what you think is good and important. For example, some people think that all-natural food is good for your health. They are likely to choose food without synthetic dyes and preservatives. These choices affect the food that companies make. Food scientists are likely to find natural materials to replace synthetic materials to meet consumer demand.

Materials Meet Needs, Desires, and Values

The stretchy material of this hair band meets the need to pull back the hair. Its color and style were chosen based on desire.

This polyester shirt meets the need for clothing. Its style reflects the desire to wear clothes that express personal tastes.

The game controller meets the desire to play video games and the value that technology should be easy to use.

5. In what ways are needs today different than they were 50 years ago?

6. Discuss Think about the plastic casing on a cell phone. Why do you think it is made of plastic? What needs, desires, or values were likely involved in its development?

Phases of the Life Cycle of Synthetic Materials

The polyester in a shirt and the plastic in a cell phone case go through many steps before they reach you. The steps that a material or product goes through are called the *life cycle* of the material. One model of a life cycle includes five steps: obtaining natural resources, production, distribution, consumer use, and disposal. The life cycle describes where a product comes from, how it is used, and where it goes after it is used.

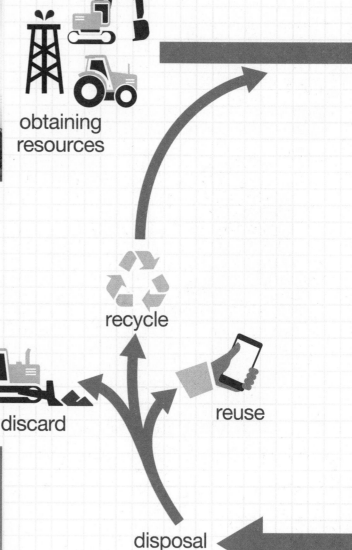

obtaining resources

recycle

discard

reuse

disposal

Obtaining Resources

The first step in a life cycle is to obtain the resources needed to make the materials. These resources may be natural resources or recycled materials. A cell phone contains many materials, including metals, plastics, and glass. The metals are produced from ores that are mined. The starting material for plastic comes from crude oil, which is extracted from the ground. Glass is made from resources such as sand and limestone.

Disposal

Consumers dispose of products when they are done using them. At this point in the life cycle, products and the materials that they contain are discarded, recycled, or reused. Products may be discarded and end up in a landfill where they remain. Some products may be flushed down the drain, where they enter the wastewater system. Many products, including plastic containers and cell phones, may be recycled to produce new materials. Other products, such as electronic devices, may be refurbished and used again.

Production

During the production stage of a synthetic material, chemical reactions or mixing processes produce the materials in the product. The materials are then shaped into the various parts of the product. Then the parts are put together to make the finished product. Cell phones may be thin, but they have many tiny parts inside the plastic covering.

production

distribution

Distribution

Products must reach consumers, but they are rarely shipped directly from the factory to the consumer. They are likely to be shipped from where they are produced to a warehouse where they are stored. From there, products may be shipped to a store or directly to the consumer.

consumer use

Consumer Use

Consumers use products in different ways. Some products, such as food and medicine, are consumed. Other products, such as a paper plate, may only be used once. Products such as cell phones may be used frequently for a long time. Products may also be shared and reused by multiple consumers.

7. Follow the arrows and label the photos to show the life cycle of a nylon rope.

WORD BANK
- consumer use
- disposal
- distribution
- obtaining resources
- production

obtaining resources

8. How else could the nylon rope be disposed of?

Natural Resource Use and Synthetic Materials

Natural resources are obtained during the first stage in the life cycle of a material or a product. However, all stages of the life cycle affect the use of natural resources. Some resources are used to make products. Other resources are used as energy resources. Consumers can reuse or recycle products to reduce the need to obtain more natural resources.

The availability of materials also affects how they are used. Some natural resources are scarce and only found in certain locations as a result of geologic processes that occurred in the past. Alternative materials that do not use those resources may be developed.

Excavators are used to harvest trees on a peatland forest on Indonesia's Borneo Island. Synthetic materials that come from trees include rayon fabric, plywood, and some rosin-based adhesives.

9. How can recycling rubber tires into materials that make playground and track surfaces affect the use of natural resources?

10. How can the end of the life cycle of a plastic bottle be the beginning of the life cycle of a polyester jacket? Record your evidence.

Language SmArts
Model the Life Cycle

11. Write a story about the life cycle of a plastic or paper shopping bag. Remember that plastic is made from petroleum and paper is made from trees.

_____

_____

_____

_____

_____

_____

_____

_____

_____

12. **Draw** In the space below, draw a diagram to model the life cycle of the plastic or paper bag.

Analyzing the Impact of Synthetic Materials

Diamonds can be a symbol of marriage or wealth for many people in the United States. In addition to being desired for their beauty, the hardness of diamonds makes them useful for industrial tasks such as cutting, grinding, drilling, and polishing. Diamonds form naturally deep within Earth, so they must be mined. An increase in the demand for diamonds means that more land must be mined.

Engineers can also make synthetic diamonds to help meet the need for diamonds. Synthetic diamonds usually cost less than natural diamonds. Also, they do not need to be mined.

13. How might the life cycle of synthetic diamonds differ from that of natural diamonds?

This thin sheet of Chemical Vapor Deposition (CVD) diamond is being held above other synthetic diamond stones. CVD diamonds can take six months to grow using methane gas and are one of the best conductors of heat in the world.

Impacts Throughout the Life Cycle

The impacts of a product containing synthetic materials can be determined by analyzing the product's life cycle. Each stage of the life cycle may have positive or negative effects on society and the environment. Producing cell phones provides people with jobs but may expose people to some materials that can cause health problems. The need to mine rare-earth minerals used in phones can harm ecosystems and cause pollution. Decisions at each stage of the life cycle can help decrease potential negative effects.

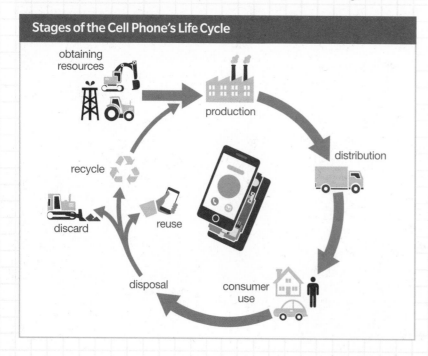

Stages of the Cell Phone's Life Cycle

obtaining resources
production
distribution
recycle
reuse
discard
consumer use
disposal

14. How might drilling for oil to make plastic used in a cell phone case impact society? Select all that apply.

A. Jobs are created for people who work for oil companies.

B. Oil spills at drilling sites can harm the environment.

C. Jobs are lost for people who produce alternative fuels.

D. Pollution from oil is reduced.

Canals are built by oil companies to move equipment.

Obtaining Resources

Mines and oil rigs are located where resources formed during past geologic processes. As these resources are harvested, the tools used and the waste created can impact the environment. For example, mining and oil drilling can pollute Earth systems. And habitats are destroyed to make way for mines or oil rigs.

On July 18, 2010, an explosion occurred at the *Deepwater Horizon* oil drilling platform. Because of the damage, an estimated 130 million gallons of oil was released into the Gulf of Mexico. The oil spill resulting from the *Deepwater Horizon* explosion affected coastal ecosystems—as shown in the photos—and deep-sea ecosystems. Many organisms died from coming in contact with the oil, and food chains were disrupted.

Obtaining oil resources alters natural cycles and does long-term damage to ecosystems in other ways too. For example, oil companies dredge canals in order to move drilling equipment. These canals destroy habitats and alter the ecosystem by changing the natural interactions of fresh and salt water. The loss of wetlands is important because wetlands protect cities like New Orleans from hurricanes. People are also affected by changes to local ecosystems. Shrimp fishing is an important job along the Gulf Coast. Shrimp depend on the wetlands ecosystem for part of their life cycle. As the wetlands are being destroyed, fewer shrimp are available as a source of food for other organisms as well as for humans.

The *Deepwater Horizon* oil drilling platform was located in the Gulf of Mexico.

Relying on natural resources can also affect the availability of a resource in the future. If we use a resource at a rate that is faster than it can be replenished, that resource will be nonrenewable. For example, the rate at which we have been using oil has depleted the supply faster than it can be replenished.

Society is affected in other ways as we obtain natural resources. For example, mining and oil drilling create jobs and provide needed resources, but these jobs can be dangerous for workers. Some people are developing renewable, and less polluting, energy resources that will also provide jobs and needed resources.

This pelican is covered in oil from the *Deepwater Horizon* oil spill.

15. How have decisions about resource use along the Gulf Coast affected local ecosystems?

Shrimping was compromised because of the spill and the fleet stayed in harbor.

Sartore/National Geographic Magazines/Getty Images; (b) ©Tom Williams/CQ-Roll Call Group/Getty Images

Production

People are employed to produce synthetic materials and then make products out of them. These jobs are often located far away from where the materials are used. For example, most cell phones are manufactured outside of the United States. Factory jobs may provide workers with new opportunities. However, factory workers in other countries may not always have the same protections as workers in the United States have. They may work very long hours for low pay or work in unsafe conditions.

Production can also cause pollution and use energy. The chemical reactions that produce synthetic materials may also produce substances that are toxic. These toxins can pollute the air, water, and ground if they are not disposed of properly. Another source of air pollution during production can be the source of energy for the factories, such as coal power plants. Burning coal releases gases and particles that contribute to air pollution.

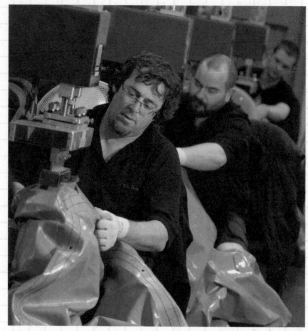

Workers in a plastics factory are making industrial strength plastic bags for use in construction.

16. What questions might an engineer ask when determining whether to produce a product from synthetic materials? Select all that apply.

    A. How are the raw materials acquired?

    B. Is there a more natural alternative that could be used?

    C. How many people will need to be employed to manufacture the material?

    D. What toxins will result if this product is manufactured?

People depend on having a safe and reliable source of fresh water for drinking as well as for manufacturing products. In some places people depend on water collected in human made reservoirs on the surface. In other places people use groundwater that has been pumped to the surface. Both sources of fresh water depend on natural patterns of rainfall to recharge.

Reservoirs and groundwater can both be contaminated when toxic materials are released during the production of synthetic materials. Some of these toxins may break down quickly, but others will continue to pollute the water supply for many years.

When people decide to produce synthetic materials they are making decisions that affect jobs as well as safety and the health of the environment. These decisions are made at the local level as well as nationally and even internationally.

Industrial waste can leak out and enter streams and infiltrate the ground.

Distribution

Today, synthetic materials and the products made from them are shipped around the world. Distribution systems are efficient and can move products to consumers quickly. Products are shipped on trucks, ships, and trains from factories to warehouses. They can also be transported to stores or directly to customers. As a result of these factors, materials and products are less expensive for consumers. However, the distribution stage also has a negative impact. It produces greenhouse gases and other pollutants as products are transported.

Many goods are transported around the world by container ship. These ships may pollute and add greenhouse gases to the atmosphere. Ship collisions are also a threat to endangered whale species.

Consumer Use

Using synthetic materials has both positive and negative effects. Many synthetic materials improve people's quality of life. For example, synthetic medicines can make people feel better and cure diseases. Cell phones help people stay connected over great distances.

Consumer use of synthetic materials can also have negative effects, which are sometimes caused by the choices consumers make. For example, people may use too much fertilizer. Excess fertilizer makes its way to streams, rivers, and oceans where it causes harmful blooms of algae.

Many products use energy and cause pollution when they are used. For example, cell phones need to be plugged in to be recharged and refrigerators constantly use energy.

Digital tablets can have a positive impact because they allow people who are far apart to communicate easily.

EVIDENCE NOTEBOOK

17. How many times does a consumer use plastic water bottles compared to how many times a person uses a new jacket? What effect does this have on all of the steps of the life cycle? Record your evidence.

Disposal

When people increase their use of materials, the amount of material that is discarded also increases. A huge amount of waste goes to landfills every day. Landfills can be smelly, which is unpleasant for people who live nearby. Improper disposal of some materials can pollute the land and water in areas near and far away from landfills. As the waste breaks down, it produces gases such as methane and carbon dioxide. The methane may be collected and burned. Some landfills are even using methane as an energy resource.

Some waste does not reach landfills, such as when people throw trash along roads or natural areas. This pollution may harm animals. Sometimes they mistake it for food. When animals eat plastic, they can die because it stays in their stomachs. Plastic can also become attached around parts of animals and cause harm to their bodies.

Reusing and recycling can reduce the materials sent to landfills. Materials are reused when they are used more than once. Consumers can also donate or share items so that someone else can use them. Recycling turns used materials into new materials that may be used again. Recycling saves energy and natural resources. It creates jobs for people who work in recycling businesses. For example, cell phone parts, such as metal and some plastics, can be recycled to make new materials. Plastic bottles can be recycled and spun into threads to make fabric.

A cell phone recycling technician works on old cell phones to recover metals and other materials that can be used again.

An employee at a cell phone company refurbishes a used cell phone that still works. The cell phone can then be resold and someone else can use it.

18. It is important for engineers to consider how a natural / synthetic material will be disposed of when they are developing the new material. If the material can be recycled / discarded, energy and natural resources could be saved. The engineer could design the material to minimize / maximize harmful environmental pollutants.

Economic Impact of the Life Cycle

A material's life cycle impacts the economy in numerous ways. All stages of a life cycle provide people with jobs. People may also work in industries that support the life cycle, such as making equipment used for mining or repairing delivery trucks. The life cycle of materials can have a big impact on the economy of countries. Some countries depend on their natural resources, such as oil. Other countries depend on the production of materials and products. Changes to the costs of natural resources or the demand for materials affects the economy. For example, low oil prices can negatively affect the economy of a country that depends on oil extraction.

Do the Math
Analyze the Economics of Recycling

Recycling helps the environment by saving energy and reducing the use of natural resources. Because materials do not need to be extracted and made from scratch, recycled materials are often less expensive to produce. The cost of natural resources, the availability of recycled materials, and the processes used to make new materials all determine whether recycling materials is economically useful. The amount of energy used in recycling compared to the amount of energy required to produce new materials is also a consideration.

Plastic water bottles can be recycled to make plastic for new products.

19. A company needs to make at least 75,000 bottles. Twenty-one 20-oz. bottles can be made from one pound of plastic. New plastic costs 83 cents/pound. Recycled plastic costs 55 cents/pound. Determine the economic impact of using new materials and recycled materials.

   The company needs _____ pounds of plastic. This much plastic will cost the company _____ if it uses new plastic and _____ if it uses recycled plastic.

20. Compare the price of the materials needed to make 75,000 bottles. Which type of plastic is the less expensive choice? How much can the company save by using the less expensive plastic?

   _____
   _____
   _____
   _____
   _____
   _____
   _____
   _____
   _____
   _____

Relating Engineering and the Life Cycle of Synthetic Materials

Engineers have shaped the life cycle of synthetic materials and the products made from them. You might realize that engineers are involved in producing cell phones. They are also involved in making simple products, such as disposable gloves and plastic bottles.

21. How can improvements that engineers make during a material's life cycle affect its impact on society and the environment?

Engineers designed this machine to test disposable gloves made from a polymer to make sure they do not leak.

Engineers Design Materials and Products

Cell phones have changed drastically since they were first invented. The first cell phones were large and could be used only to talk. Cell phones today are thin, sleek, and can be used to talk and text. They can also do almost anything a computer can do. These changes are the result of improvements that engineers made at some stages of a cell phone's life cycle. To improve cell phones, engineers define the criteria and constraints of a problem. These include the costs, safety, energy usage, potential pollution, and how the material needs to work. They find solutions by analyzing and testing possible solutions.

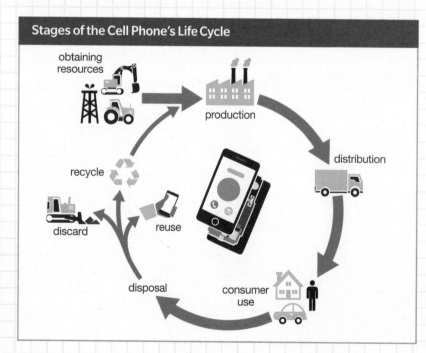

Stages of the Cell Phone's Life Cycle

obtaining resources — production — distribution — consumer use — disposal — discard — reuse — recycle

22. Discuss What roles might engineers play in the life cycle of a material? Discuss how they might be involved in extracting materials, making and improving materials and products, improving distribution, and sorting recyclables.

Obtaining Resources

Engineers develop and improve ways of finding and extracting natural resources. They design tools that are used to drill for oil. They have developed new ways of extracting natural gas. These processes provide access to resources that could not be extracted in the past.

One way to extract oil is by hydraulic fracturing, commonly called "fracking." This process involves drilling down to a rock layer that contains oil and injecting a mixture of chemicals at high pressure. The rock fractures, and the oil can then be pumped to the surface. The long-term effects on the groundwater and on the stability of the rock in the area need to be considered along with the benefits that can come from new sources of oil.

This drilling rig is used as part of a hydraulic fracturing operation.

23. It is important to know what *natural gases / chemicals* are being used in hydraulic fracturing operations that are near sources of groundwater. If the chemicals are toxic, they may contaminate the groundwater and may *harm / benefit* people who consume the groundwater.

Production

Engineers play many roles in the production of synthetic materials. They oversee the production process. Engineers look for ways to make processes more efficient and cheaper. They figure out ways to minimize waste materials. Engineers also design and improve machines, like the one in the photo. Engineers are also helping to develop and improve renewable resources, including solar and wind energy.

This machine turns melted plastic into many plastic pieces that are all the same shape.

Distribution

Traditional distribution processes include shipping by sea, air, and road. Engineers have been inventing new, "eco-friendly" packaging materials and new ways to use traditional materials. Synthetic materials are involved in the distribution of products in the form of protective packaging, such as packing "peanuts." Engineers are working to help make the processes involved with distribution more efficient. Some companies are considering using drones to deliver their products directly to their customers. The air space above us is a natural resource, and decisions will have to be made about how this resource can be shared. Engineers will have many problems to solve in order to make sure that commercial drones can operate safely.

24. What are some of the problems engineers will have to solve so that commercial drones can deliver products to your home?

Drones can be used to deliver products.

Consumer Use

Engineers design products to meet the needs and values of consumers. For example, consumers expressed concern about carbon dioxide emissions from gas-powered cars. Engineers worked with scientists to design cars that use less fuel and produce fewer pollutants. As a result, new hybrid cars run on batteries part of the time, and electric cars only use batteries. While battery powered and electric cars reduce or eliminate the need for gas, they still rely on a source of energy to charge their batteries. This energy may come from the sun through solar panels, or from the wind through wind turbines. Both of these technologies use materials that can have long-term effects on the environment.

Solar panels require a lot of space to generate enough energy to meet the needs they were designed to fill.

25. How might using a large area of land for solar panels have a negative effect on a local ecosystem? Select all that apply.

   A. Solar panels can provide energy without creating pollution.

   B. Using land for solar panels disrupts the habitats in the ecosystem.

   C. Solar panels can prevent plants from growing by blocking sunlight from reaching the ground.

   D. Installing solar panels provides jobs for people.

Disposal

While many synthetic materials end up in landfills, or in the oceans, the disposal of natural and synthetic materials can be engineered. For example, engineers have helped improve product packaging so that it has less impact on the environment. Polystyrene foam packing peanuts were once widely used to cushion objects during shipping. The peanuts can be reused, but they cannot be easily recycled. Engineers have developed air-filled plastic pouches and packaging peanuts made out of cornstarch to replace the plastic foam peanuts. These *biodegradable* materials break down without leaving hazardous waste.

Food packaging can be made from corn, soy, or sugar cane, which are biodegradable.

Engineers play an important role in the recycling of materials. Materials that can be recycled include metals, glass, paper, and many types of plastic. Not only do the different types of materials need to be separated, the different types of plastics also need to be separated from each other. Engineers have developed methods to separate and clean recycled materials. The materials can then be shredded or melted to make new products.

26. **Discuss** Why is it important for engineers to consider the entire life cycle of the materials they use when they design new products?

Hands-On Lab
Sort Synthetic Materials Using Properties

You will design a process to separate materials.

You can use only the physical properties of the materials, such as density and attraction to a magnet. Imagine your materials will be going directly from one step to another step. You cannot sort them by picking out the parts by hand. You may make screens with holes in them using scissors and cardboard.

MATERIALS
- bowl of water
- cardboard
- fan
- fine mesh sieve
- magnet
- materials to sort: marbles, metal paper clips, small balls of aluminum foil, plastic straws, pieces of paper
- scissors

Sorting Machine at Recycling Plant

People do sort some materials in recycling centers, but machines do a large part of the sorting based on the properties of the materials.

Procedure

STEP 1 Identify the criteria and constraints of the sorting process. Record your notes.

STEP 2 Discuss the properties of the materials and how you might use them to sort the materials. Record your conclusions.

STEP 3 Design a process to sort the materials. Describe your process.

STEP 4 Make a model to test your sorting process. Record your results.

STEP 5 Record any limitations you discovered in your solution. Revise your sorting process as needed to solve any problems you encountered during your tests. Record the changes you make to your process. Record the results of tests using your modified sorting process.

Analysis

STEP 6 Which methods were successful for separating materials by their physical properties, and which methods did not work as expected?

STEP 7 Prepare a presentation for the class to demonstrate how you sorted the materials.

Engineer It
Analyze the Life Cycle of Carbon Fibers

Carbon fiber is a strong synthetic material that has low weight, can resist chemicals, and can withstand high temperatures. It is used in products, such as windmill blades, airplane brakes, and racecar bodies. The process by which carbon fibers are made is relatively expensive because it requires a large amount of energy. The materials must go through several steps of manufacturing, including heating and stretching.

27. Explain how engineers might work to improve the production or consumer use of carbon fiber.

_____

_____

_____

_____

_____

_____

_____

EVIDENCE NOTEBOOK

28. At what stage(s) in the life cycle of a plastic bottle could engineers prepare the bottles to become a jacket? Record your evidence.

Continue Your Exploration

Name: _____   Date: _____

Check out the path below or go online to choose one of the other paths shown.

> **Careers in Engineering**
>
> - **Researching Life Cycles**
> - **Hands-On Labs** ✋
> - **Propose Your Own Path**
>
> *Go online to choose one of these other paths.*

Materials Engineer

Materials engineers study how a material's properties are related to its structure. They learn how processing affects the material's properties. Materials engineers develop new materials with specific properties that are suited to their applications. They also develop processes to make these materials, and they test the materials' properties.

Materials engineers work on many kinds of materials in many different products, such as new materials that allow cell phones to work faster or store more information. They make materials that help to restore and protect art. They develop materials that are used inside the body to treat medical conditions. Materials engineers even help protect the environment. They can develop materials that can detect and remove toxic chemicals from water. They are also finding ways to make biodegradable plastics.

This engineer is preparing liquid glass for use in bone implant research. When hardened into foam, the bioactive glass is used as a scaffold for growing human bone.

Continue Your Exploration

1. A materials engineer is developing new materials that can withstand high-heat environments, such as rocket engines. How might understanding the chemical makeup and properties of materials help the engineer design these materials?

2. People with severe burns need their skin to heal. They often require skin grafts to cover burned areas until they heal. However, the burns can sometimes be too extensive to use the patient's own tissue for the graft. How might this need of burn patients drive materials engineers to design new materials?

3. When boats transporting oil crash or run aground, the water can become polluted with large amounts of crude oil. Because the density of oil is less than that of water, the oil will remain on the water's surface. The oil can then spread and be moved around by water movement and wind. If you were a materials engineer, how might you design a material that could contain the spill and remove as much of the oil from the water as possible?

4. **Collaborate** With a partner, discuss how materials engineers might be involved in the development of synthetic diamonds. What might drive them to want to make diamonds? How might they develop a process to make them? Create a flow chart that shows the life cycle of a synthetic diamond, from inspiration to final product.

Can You Explain It?

Name: _____ Date: _____

> **How can engineers change the effects of the synthetic materials in the bottles on the environment by reusing the materials to make the jacket?**

EVIDENCE NOTEBOOK

Refer to the notes in your Evidence Notebook to help you construct an explanation for how engineers can change the effects of the synthetic material in the bottles on the environment by reusing the material to make the jacket.

1. State your claim. Make sure your claim fully explains how engineers can change the effects of the synthetic materials in the plastic bottles on the environment by reusing the materials to make the jacket.

2. Summarize the evidence you have gathered to support your claim and explain your reasoning.

Checkpoints

Answer the following questions to check your understanding of the lesson.

Use the photo to answer Questions 3–4.

3. Which stages of the life cycle of the bowl happen directly before and directly after the stage shown in the photo? Select all that apply.

   A. The production stage happens immediately before.

   B. The distribution stage happens immediately before.

   C. The disposal stage happens immediately after.

   D. The obtaining resources stage happens immediately after.

4. The production of the plastic bowl is driven by the *desire / need* to have products to prepare food. The color of the bowl reflects the *desire / value* to have decorative, functional items. The use of the bowl could reflect the *need / value* that home cooked meals are better than fast food.

Use the photo to answer Questions 5–6.

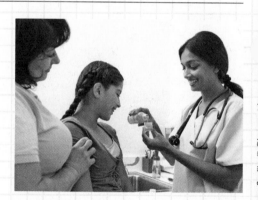

5. What is a positive impact on society of the synthetic material being consumed in the photo?

   A. Pollution is likely reduced.

   B. Human health is likely improved.

   C. Natural resources are likely conserved.

   D. Carbon dioxide emissions are likely reduced.

6. How are engineers likely to affect the life cycle of a synthetic medicine? Select all that apply.

   A. by optimizing reaction conditions to reduce the cost of making the medicine

   B. by developing ways to package the medicine so that it cannot be opened by children

   C. by determining the price of the medicine to maximize the profit for the company

   D. by regulating the medicine so that it must be prescribed by doctors

---

7. What negative impact might a factory that produces plastic products have on a local ecosystem? Select all that apply.

   A. Waste from the factory may alter the life cycles of some of the organisms in the ecosystem.

   B. More people from the local area will be employed at the factory.

   C. More roads will be built in the area helping to fragment habitats.

   D. Waste from the factory may be recycled to produce fertilizers for plants in the ecosystem.

Interactive Review

Complete this section to review the main concepts of the lesson.

Synthetic materials are developed based on consumers' needs, wants, and desires. A five-stage life cycle is one way to model all the ways in which synthetic materials and products can affect society.

A. Make a sketch to show the life cycle of a synthetic material.

Each stage of the life cycle of a material can have positive and negative effects on the environment and society.

B. Explain two positive and two negative effects that synthetic materials could have on society.

Engineers are involved in all stages of the life cycle of synthetic materials.

C. Give an example of the type of improvement an engineer could design for two stages of the life cycle of a synthetic product.

Choose one of the activities to explore how this unit connects to other topics.

☐ People in Engineering

Dr. Elizabeth Cochran, Geophysicist

Dr. Cochran studies fault zones and ways to monitor earthquakes to better understand the timing and location of earthquakes and how to minimize risks to human populations. Cochran was awarded the Presidential Early Career Awards for Scientists and Engineers for her work on the Quake-Catcher Network, a citizen-science initiative that monitors seismic activity using volunteers' computers.

Research a natural hazard citizen science project, such as the Quake-Catcher Network, that you can participate in individually or as a class. Create a short presentation that describes the objective and methods of the project and your experiences participating in the project.

☐ Life Science Connection

Effects of Plastics on Animals Many animals will be exposed to one or more human-made chemicals in their lifetimes. Many of these chemicals are found in plastic products or are byproducts of plastic manufacturing.

Choose an animal species that has been especially affected by the manufacture and use of plastics. Create an oral presentation of your findings to deliver to your class. Describe how society could help your chosen animal by reducing the effects of harmful chemicals found in plastics.

☐ Health Connection

Natural Disasters and Disease When natural disasters happen, many people lose access to resources such as fresh water and to services such as water and proper sanitation. Without the ability to stay clean and get rid of wastes, people are increasingly likely to become sick.

Research how natural disasters can affect a community's quality of life. Using Hurricane Maria as a case study, analyze how natural disasters can lead to disease outbreaks. Identify ways that this effect of natural hazards could be mitigated. Prepare a multimedia presentation to summarize your findings.

Name: _____   Date: _____

Use the photograph of the river delta to answer Questions 1–2.

1. At the mouth of a slow-flowing river, a broad, flat delta can form, often extending many kilometers into the sea. Which geologic processes are responsible for the formation of a river delta? Select all that apply.

   A. weathering

   B. erosion

   C. deposition

   D. plate movement

2. What information would you need to determine what natural hazards might affect this region? Select all that apply.

   A. the amount of rainfall it receives

   B. the size of the human population

   C. the distance to the nearest plate boundary

   D. the type of rock that makes up the surface

Use the information provided in the graph to answer Questions 3–4.

3. Between 1900 and 2004, the amount of property damage caused by hurricanes has *increased / decreased* and the number of deaths caused by hurricanes has *increased / decreased*.

4. Which of these factors most likely account for the trends in hurricane damage and deaths over time? Circle all that apply.

   A. decrease in human population in hurricane-prone areas

   B. increase in number of structures in hurricane paths

   C. change in the locations where hurricanes happen

   D. change in the conditions that cause hurricanes

   E. changes in monitoring and forecasting technology

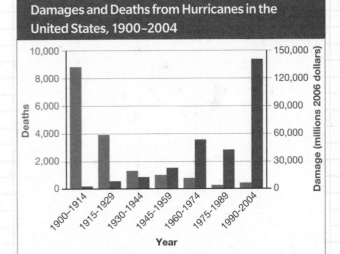

Damages and Deaths from Hurricanes in the United States, 1900–2004

Source: Blake et al., *The Deadliest, Costliest, and Most Intense United States Tropical Cyclones from 1851 to 2006 (and Other Frequently Requested Hurricane Facts)*, NOAA Technical Memorandum NWS TPC-5, updated April 2007

5. As part of the *response to / recovery from* a wildfire, synthetic material combined with water can be dropped on the fire from an airplane.

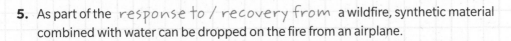

6. Complete the table by providing at least one example of how these events or processes relate to each big concept.

Hazard or Process	Time and Spatial Scales	Stability and Change	Patterns
Flood			
Earthquake			
Landslide			
Disposal of plastic shopping bag			

Name: _____   **Date:** _____

Use the map to answer Questions 7–11.

7. Which regions of Florida have the most sinkholes?

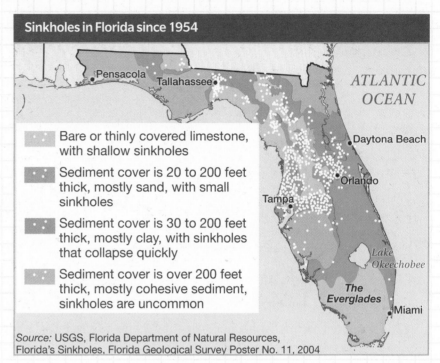

Sinkholes in Florida since 1954

Bare or thinly covered limestone, with shallow sinkholes

Sediment cover is 20 to 200 feet thick, mostly sand, with small sinkholes

Sediment cover is 30 to 200 feet thick, mostly clay, with sinkholes that collapse quickly

Sediment cover is over 200 feet thick, mostly cohesive sediment, sinkholes are uncommon

Source: USGS, Florida Department of Natural Resources, Florida's Sinkholes, Florida Geological Survey Poster No. 11, 2004

8. What types of sinkholes form most often in each type of rock or soil?

9. What types of monitoring technology and/or precursor events (if any) could be used to forecast sinkhole formation?

10. What would people in Florida need to know in order to develop mitigation protocols for the type of sinkholes that form in a given area? How might mitigation plans differ for people in Pensacola and Orlando?

11. How might synthetic materials be used as part of a sinkhole mitigation plan?

Use the diagram to answer Questions 12–15.

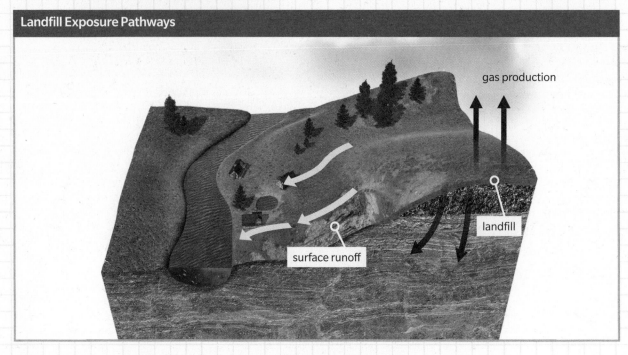

Landfill Exposure Pathways

gas production

landfill

surface runoff

12. How might each of Earth's four main subsystems be affected when synthetic materials escape from a landfill?

13. What are some decisions that could be made to reduce the environmental impacts of materials in landfills?

14. What kinds of natural disaster could change the rate at which the waste materials in the landfill enter the surrounding ecosystem?

15. How might the material leaking out of the landfill affect humans living downstream many years after the landfill is closed?

Name: Date:

What is the best plan to improve a park?

Imagine you are on a task force making plans to improve a park near Halls Bayou in Houston, Texas. A bayou is a sluggish stream or river. You want to add features to an existing park for people to enjoy, such as picnic pavilions, playgrounds, soccer fields, a stage, and walking and jogging trails. However, the area is at risk of seasonal flooding. Analyze information about the risk of flooding and use that information to develop a map of your proposed park improvements and a plan for minimizing any flood damage.

Halls Bayou Flood Map

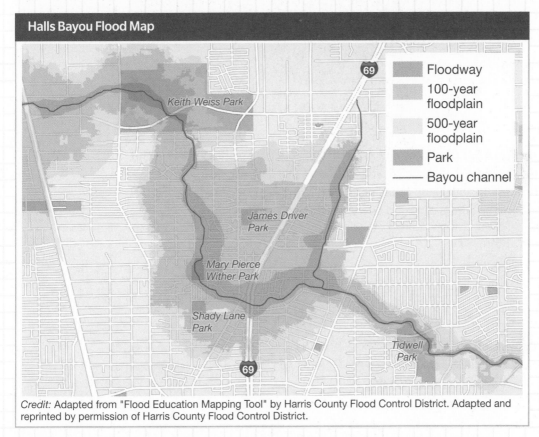

Credit: Adapted from "Flood Education Mapping Tool" by Harris County Flood Control District. Adapted and reprinted by permission of Harris County Flood Control District.

The steps below will help guide your research and will help you propose a map of the new park features and a plan to mitigate the effects of flooding.

Engineer It

1. **Ask a Question** What information do you need to know in order to develop your plan?

Engineer It

2. **Conduct Research** Research the meaning of the different zones on the map: *channel, floodway, 100-year floodplain,* and *500-year floodplain.*

3. **Analyze and Interpret Data** Using past data on floods in this area, determine which areas are more or less likely to flood. Choose one of the existing parks in the area to develop by adding your proposed features.

4. **Design a Solution** Consider how each of your park features will respond to flooding. Create a map of your park plan that includes the proposed park features. Include flood zone information in the map, and identify ways to reduce the effects of a flood on the park's features.

5. **Communicate** Present your map and park plan to the class. Explain how you chose the placement of your park's features and how your park is designed to minimize the effects of flooding.

Self-Check

	I conducted research about what different flood risk zones mean.
	I analyzed and interpreted data about flood risk, topography, and construction constraints.
	I designed a solution for building park structures in a flood-prone area.
	I clearly communicated my solution to others.

Biodiversity and Ecosystem Dynamics

How can humans sustain biodiversity and ecosystem services?

The size and salt level of the Great Salt Lake in Utah change over time. As water evaporates, salt deposits are left behind.

You Solve It Why are Adélie penguin population sizes changing?

Investigate changing penguin populations in Antarctica by analyzing maps and data about climate, food, feeding behaviors, and penguins.

Go online and complete the You Solve It to explore ways to solve a real-world problem.

523

Evaluate Biodiversity Design Solutions

This cougar, known as P-22, lives in Griffith Park in Los Angeles. U.S. Route 101 divides cougar habitat in southern California, reducing the animals' natural hunting and breeding range.

A. Look at the photo. On a separate sheet of paper, write down as many different questions as you can about the photo.

B. Discuss With your class or a partner, share your questions. Record any additional questions generated in your discussion. Then choose the most important questions from the list that are related to maintaining biodiversity. Write them below.

C. Choose a problem related to biodiversity loss in your area or in another location to research. Here's a list of problems you can consider:

- extinction of wild native crows on Mauna Loa in Hawaii
- deforestation of Europe
- coral reef bleaching
- local extinction of wild lynx in Colorado
- introduction of mongoose populations in Hawaii
- feral cat populations

What problem related to biodiversity loss will you research?

D. Use the information above, along with your research, to evaluate design solutions for the biodiversity problem you choose.

 Discuss the next steps for your Unit Project with your teacher and go online to download the Unit Project Worksheet.

UNIT 7

Language Development

Use the lessons in this unit to complete the network and expand your understanding of these key concepts.

- Similar term
- Phrase
- Cognate
- Example
- Definition

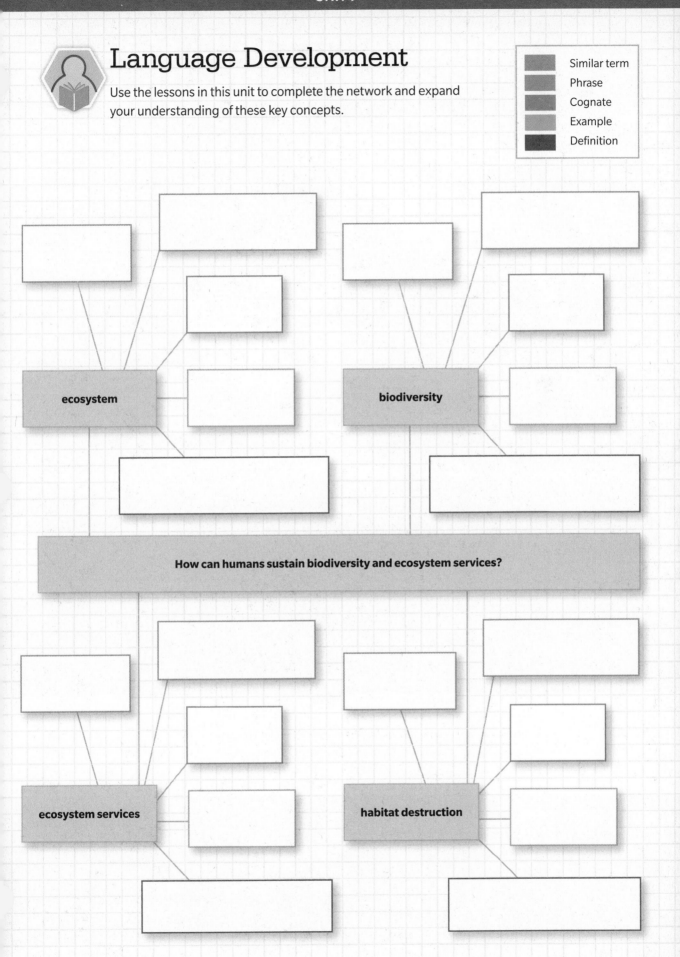

ecosystem

biodiversity

How can humans sustain biodiversity and ecosystem services?

ecosystem services

habitat destruction

Biodiversity Indicates Ecosystem Health

This coral reef ecosystem in Thailand is home to a large number and variety of animals and other organisms.

Explore First

Modeling Ecosystem Change What contributes to an ecosystem's ability to recover from change? Model an ecosystem by using colored blocks to build a structure. Each color represents a different part of the ecosystem. What happens when you remove all the blocks of one color? How could you change this outcome?

Go online to view the digital version of the Hands-On Lab for this lesson and to download additional lab resources.

CAN YOU EXPLAIN IT?

What factors might influence how this ecosystem would recover from such a large and sudden flood?

before flood

during flood

Several days of heavy rains caused the Vltava River in the Czech Republic to flood extensively in 2002. Towns and cities as well as the natural environment were all affected by this sudden disturbance. Some areas recovered more quickly than others.

1. Study the two photos. Construct a cause-and-effect statement about how the flooding likely affected this ecosystem.

2. What types of living things do you think were the first to return or regrow after the floodwaters receded?

EVIDENCE NOTEBOOK As you explore this lesson, gather evidence to help explain what factors might influence this ecosystem's recovery after a flood.

Getty Images

Describing Biodiversity

Forests, salt marshes, deserts, and lakes are all examples of ecosystems. An ecosystem can be a small pond or extend across a vast grassland. Although there are many different types of ecosystems, they all have some common features. An **ecosystem** is a system made up of all the living and nonliving things in a given area. The living parts of an ecosystem interact with each other and with nonliving parts. Because of these interactions, ecosystems are dynamic—they are always changing. For example, the living components shown in the photos constantly interact with the nonliving and other living components. The macaques, a type of monkey, take in oxygen by breathing air and eat mostly plants and insects. The sea stars take in oxygen from the water through their feet and eat mostly mollusks.

This land ecosystem in Morocco contains several populations of organisms, including the endangered Barbary macaque. Macaques live alongside humans in certain parts of Morocco.

This marine ecosystem also contains several populations of organisms, including sea stars and mollusks. They live alongside many types of fish and coral in this ecosystem.

3. Fill in the table by listing the components in the word bank as living or nonliving parts of the ecosystems in the photos.

Living	Nonliving
	water

WORD BANK
- ~~water~~
- plants
- sand
- air
- fish
- rocks
- macaques
- algae

Biodiversity

One way to evaluate the health of an ecosystem is to consider its biodiversity. **Biodiversity** refers to the variety of life in Earth's land, freshwater, and marine ecosystems. Biodiversity can be studied at different scales. Scales can range from a small area, such as a drop of water, to a large area, such as a forest. An area's biodiversity may be made up of a few species or thousands of species. High biodiversity exists when there are many species and individuals of those species living in an ecosystem. Low biodiversity exists when there is a low number of species in an ecosystem. The biodiversity of an area can be described as the combination of genetic diversity, species diversity, and ecosystem diversity.

Levels of Biodiversity

Genetic diversity refers to the variation of genes within a species or population in a given area. For example, the coyotes living in this prairie may vary in body size, leg length, fur color, or other characteristics. These characteristics are encoded by genes, which are passed from generation to generation. All the possible genetic variations of the coyotes in this prairie make up the population's genetic diversity.

Species diversity refers to both the number of different species that are in a given area and the number of individuals of each species that are there. In this prairie, you can see a variety of plants and animals. If you could see more of this ecosystem, you would most likely see more species. These species interact with each other and with the nonliving parts of the prairie ecosystem.

Ecosystem diversity refers to the variety of ecosystems in a given area. Ecosystem diversity refers to both land and aquatic ecosystems. For example, the area shown here contains several types of ecosystems, including a stream, a prairie, and a riverbank. Ecosystems may be large or very small.

4. Which statement best describes an example of low species diversity?

   A. A population of chorus frogs has a wide variety of skin colors.

   B. A marsh ecosystem is covered by a single species of cattail bulrushes.

   C. A state park includes multiple forest, wetland, and freshwater ecosystems.

Hands-On Lab
Measure Biodiversity

Conduct a simulated measurement of two types of biodiversity: species richness and species abundance.

Bumblebees are important pollinators of plants and crops. Humans rely on them to pollinate food crops. Suppose you are surveying bumblebees within a tall-grass prairie ecosystem. Your job is to provide an estimate of their biodiversity.

Tricolor bumblebees nest underground in colonies.

Procedure and Analysis

STEP 1 Observe the jar of beans. It is a model of the bumblebee population found in a tall-grass prairie ecosystem. The different bean types represent the different bumblebee species. Decide which bean type will represent each species and record this information in the table.

MATERIALS
- large jar of dried beans (6 different types)
- scoop or cup

STEP 2 Take a full scoop of beans from the jar. These beans represent individual bumblebees from your sample area.

STEP 3 *Species richness* refers to the number of different species found in a given area. What is the species richness of your sample area?

STEP 4 *Species abundance* refers to the number of individuals of each species found in a given area. Record in the table the species abundance for each species found in your sample area.

STEP 5 **Do the Math** Determine the relative species abundance for each species in the sample area. Relative species abundance will be reported as a percentage. Record your data in the table.

$$\text{Relative abundance} = \frac{\text{species abundance}}{\text{total number of bumblebees in sample}} \times 100$$

Data for Sample Area			
Bumblebee species	Bean type	Species abundance	Relative abundance
Common eastern			
Rusty patched			
American			
Two-spotted			
Tricolored			
Brown-belted			

STEP 6 Draw a second table on a sheet of paper and combine your data with the data from the rest of the class. What is the species richness, according to class data?

STEP 7 Record species abundance in the class data table. Calculate and record relative species abundance using the overall class data.

STEP 8 How did your data differ from the overall class data? What might account for any differences? Discuss these questions in small groups. Then share ideas and listen to others in a whole-class discussion.

STEP 9 Develop hypotheses about the size of the scoop of beans you would need to be able to accurately measure different types of biodiversity and to sample rare bumblebee species in the ecosystem.

Identify Patterns in Biodiversity

A variety of factors, including location, climate, and resource availability, can affect an ecosystem's biodiversity. Certain regions of Earth have very high biodiversity compared to other regions. Some of these regions have been identified as biodiversity hotspots. A *biodiversity hotspot* is a region that has high biodiversity and is threatened with possible destruction. Some land and marine hotspots are identified on the map.

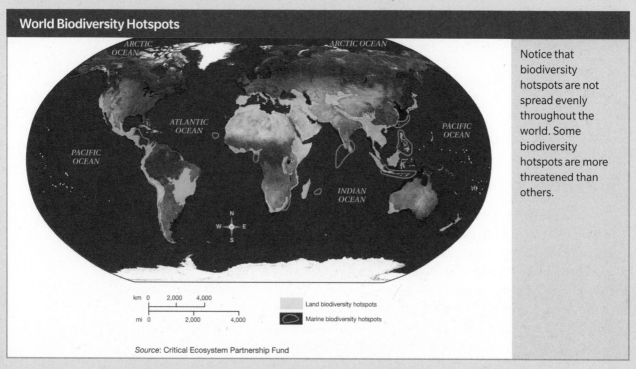

World Biodiversity Hotspots

Notice that biodiversity hotspots are not spread evenly throughout the world. Some biodiversity hotspots are more threatened than others.

km 0   2,000   4,000
mi 0   2,000   4,000

Land biodiversity hotspots
Marine biodiversity hotspots

Source: Critical Ecosystem Partnership Fund

5. Biodiversity hotspots are common near the equator / poles.
Hotspots include ecosystems on land only / land and in water.

Evaluating Ecosystem Health

Changes to an ecosystem can affect how the parts of an ecosystem interact. Within a healthy ecosystem, however, factors stay more or less within a certain range and in a mostly stable condition, even as individual parts change. Ecologists call this phenomenon *ecosystem stability*. Recall that matter and energy flow among the living and nonliving parts of an ecosystem. A change to any part of an ecosystem may disrupt the flow of energy and matter.

Ecosystem Interactions Include the Flow of Energy and Matter

Sunlight is the original source of energy in this desert ecosystem.

Plants use energy from sunlight to transform water and carbon dioxide into sugars and oxygen during photosynthesis. The plants take in water from the soil and carbon dioxide from the air. They use the sugars they make as food.

These burros eat plants in the Sonoran desert. Energy and matter move from the plants into the burros.

6. Suppose a new animal is introduced into this desert ecosystem. The animal has no natural predators. It eats the same plants the wild burros do. Which parts of the ecosystem might be affected by this change? Choose all that apply.

   A. other animals

   B. plants

   C. flow of energy

   D. cycling of matter

Disturbances in Ecosystems

An *ecosystem disturbance* is a change in environmental conditions that causes a change in an ecosystem. Both living and nonliving parts of an ecosystem can be affected by a disturbance. Natural disturbances include wildfires, storms, flooding, tsunamis, and volcanic eruptions. Sudden increases in animal populations, such as insect swarms, can also cause a disturbance. Humans can also create ecosystem disturbances. These changes include oil spills, fires, and the clearing of land to harvest trees. Humans also clear land to make space for agriculture, housing, roads, or industry. The removal or introduction of a species in an area also creates a disturbance. Ecosystems can recover from disturbances. How quickly an ecosystem recovers depends on the type and severity of the disturbance.

An Ecosystem Disturbance

A landslide greatly affected this ecosystem in the Philippines. The land was covered by mud and rocks that removed plants and displaced people and other animals.

This photo shows the same ecosystem just one year after the landslide. Plants are growing on the landslide mud. Animals and people have returned to live in the area.

The biodiversity of an ecosystem that experiences a disturbance can influence how well the ecosystem recovers. Ecosystems with high biodiversity have many species fulfilling certain roles, such as pollinator, decomposer, and predator. The graphic below shows how ecosystems with high and low biodiversity can be affected by disturbances.

Biodiversity Impacts Ecosystem Stability

This graphic models the stability of four different ecosystems during years with different amounts of rainfall. The different-colored dots represent different species of insect pollinators. Some of these insects do better in high-rainfall years. Others do better in low-rainfall years.

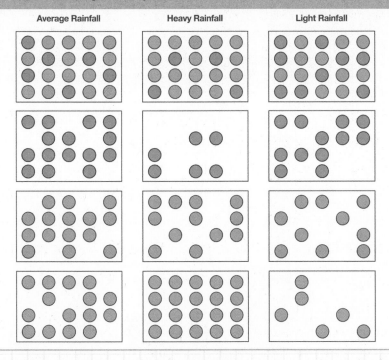

Diverse community Some species do better in wetter years. Others do better in drier years. The total number of pollinators remains stable.

Community made up mostly of red species This pollinator species is negatively affected by high rainfall.

Community made up of mostly green species This pollinator species does poorly in wetter and drier years.

Community made up of mostly blue species This pollinator species is negatively affected by low rainfall.

7. In your own words, explain how rainfall could influence the species abundance over time in the different communities. In which ecosystem is the least amount of change observed in the abundance of pollinators?

Biodiversity and Ecosystem Health

The health of an ecosystem includes its ability to recover from a disturbance. Ecological diversity, species diversity, and genetic diversity all contribute to ecosystem stability. A diverse ecosystem has more ways to recover from a disturbance. If one species dies or leaves a diverse ecosystem, another species can take its place. As a result, the ecosystem can stabilize more quickly.

An ecosystem with lowered biodiversity is less able to recover from a disturbance. Some ecosystems, such as those in polar regions, can maintain stability while naturally having lower biodiversity than warmer regions. Ecosystems generally become less stable when their biodiversity levels are lowered from their baseline levels.

EVIDENCE NOTEBOOK

8. How would biodiversity levels affect the recovery of ecosystems along the Vltava River after the floodwaters recede? Record your evidence.

Do the Math
Assess Ecosystem Health

Having many different species in an ecosystem is a sign of high species diversity. But the size of each population of species is also important. A population can be too small. Fewer individuals means there is less genetic diversity in a population. The graph shows the biodiversity of birds in two ecosystems. Both ecosystems have an equal amount of species diversity. However, they are different in some significant ways.

9. What are the main differences in species abundance between the populations of birds in the two ecosystems?

10. Given the data in the graph, what can you predict about how each ecosystem might recover from a disturbance?

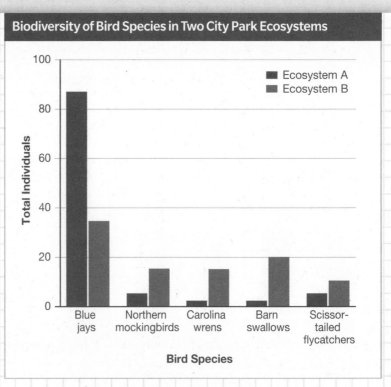

Biodiversity of Bird Species in Two City Park Ecosystems

Analyzing Human Influences on Biodiversity

Humans have designed structures and developed processes that help them survive in their environments. Ecosystems provide the energy and raw materials that humans need to live and survive. For example, we use wood from trees to build homes. We burn wood and fossil fuels to provide energy. Humans rely on ecosystems to grow crops and raise livestock. Humans also depend on the nonliving parts of ecosystems for clean air, fresh water, and living space. In this way, humans can also affect the health and biodiversity of different ecosystems.

Humans introduced the European honeybee (*Apis mellifera*) to North America. These bees make honey and beeswax.

11. Humans rely on certain services that ecosystems provide. Which ecosystem processes below do humans benefit from? Circle all that apply.

A. decomposition of wastes

B. pollination of crops

C. filtering of fresh water

D. growth of trees and plants

Humans Are Part of Earth's Ecosystems

Humans rely on and can influence ecosystems. We depend on healthy ecosystems for survival and for a good quality of life. For example, every time you breathe or drink a glass of water, you depend on ecosystem processes to provide oxygen and fresh, clean water. Healthy ecosystems buffer the impact of storms, limit the spread of disease, and recycle nutrients. Humans rely on ecosystems to reduce the effects of droughts and floods, provide fertile soils, pollinate crops and plants, disperse seeds, and control pests by natural predators. These beneficial functions depend on ecosystem health, which is often measured by the integrity of an ecosystem's biodiversity. For these reasons and more, high biodiversity in ecosystems is important to all humans.

Negative Impacts on Biodiversity

Human activities affect the biodiversity of ecosystems. Although we rely on healthy ecosystems, many human activities negatively affect biodiversity. Some activities cause direct negative effects, such as overharvesting of plants or animals. Other activities cause indirect negative effects. For example, constructing new buildings can destroy habitats and reduce biodiversity. Releasing garbage and pollution into the environment can harm or poison organisms and reduce biodiversity.

Habitat Destruction

Activities such as the construction of roads, buildings, towns, and cities cause habitat destruction. Mining and harvesting resources also remove habitats. Less habitat means less biodiversity at all levels—ecosystem, species, and genetic. Human activity can also break large habitats into smaller pieces. When a habitat is broken into smaller pieces, animals that need a large area of habitat can no longer live there.

Introduced Species

Tulips, orange trees, and many other highly valued plants are now grown in the United States. However, they are not native to the country. People introduced them to a new environment when they brought them from other countries. These nonnative species are called *introduced species*. Introduced species can have negative impacts on ecosystems. For example, buckthorn, lionfish, emerald ash borers, and Burmese pythons are invasive organisms that threaten native species in several North American ecosystems. These species do not have predators or other natural factors in their new environments that limit their populations' growth.

Overharvested Species

Many fish species are harvested for food. The overharvesting of certain fish species threatens marine biodiversity. For example, decades of overfishing led to an extreme drop in populations of Atlantic cod in the early 1990s. This almost caused the collapse of the cod fishing industry. The fishing of Atlantic cod in the north Atlantic was banned in 1992. Overharvesting of plants such as coneflower and American ginseng has greatly reduced their wild population sizes. Land animal species, such as bison, have also been hunted to near extinction. When a population is reduced to a very small size due to overharvesting, genetic diversity is lost.

Habitat destruction occurs when land is cleared for development.

Pet Burmese pythons that were released into the wild threaten biodiversity in areas of South Florida.

Atlantic cod populations are closely monitored and are slowly recovering from near extinction in the early 1990s.

Lack of Biodiversity in Food Crops

Many of today's food crops have very little genetic diversity. Some crops, such as bananas, are all genetically identical. Recall that genetic diversity in a population increases the likelihood that some members of a population will survive a disturbance such as a disease. Genetically identical food crops are more likely to be destroyed by a disturbance because every plant reacts in the same way. In the case of bananas, a fungal disease, called *Panama disease,* is destroying banana plants. This disease is threatening banana crops and the livelihood of the people who grow and sell them.

Scientists are working on reintroducing into crops some of the wild-type genes that were lost during domestication. The intention of this bioengineering is to make hardier crops. The wild cousins of crop plants tend to be better able to survive disturbances. Scientists hope that reintroducing wild genes into crop plants will create crops that are more pest and drought resistant and better able to take in nutrients from the soil.

 EVIDENCE NOTEBOOK

12. Look at the image of the ecosystem before the flood. What evidence of human influence do you see, and how might this affect the ecosystem's recovery after the flood? Record your evidence.

Efforts to Protect Biodiversity

Not all human activities negatively affect biodiversity. Around the globe, people are working to limit the negative impact of human activity and preserve biodiversity. In many locations, nature preserves have been created to protect habitats. Wildlife corridors have been created to connect areas of natural habitat divided by roads or development. Awareness of overharvesting has also become more common. This awareness promotes policies to prevent additional overharvesting and guide the recovery of populations. One way plant biodiversity has been supported is by creating seed banks around the world. These banks help preserve biodiversity by storing different types of plant seeds. Seed banks are a resource for plant breeders.

This forest is managed in a way that provides a sustainable source of wood for industry.

 13. Language SmArts Construct an argument about why people should work toward having positive influences on biodiversity. Support your claims with clear reasons and relevant evidence. Present your argument to the class.

Engineer It
Monitor and Preserve Biodiversity

Disrupting any part of an ecosystem can change its biodiversity. Suppose a builder clears a field to build houses. In the field, several wildflower species grow. Different animal species living in and around the field depended on the wildflowers for food. Without the food source, those species would die or move away.

Measuring biodiversity before and after a disturbance is one way to monitor changes in an ecosystem. For example, biodiversity counts can be taken before the field is cleared and again after the houses are built. Comparing these counts helps determine the effects the disturbance had on the health of the area. Solutions can be incorporated into building designs to help preserve and protect biodiversity that may be affected by a development.

14. How might biodiversity data be used to design a solution for maintaining biodiversity at a new housing development?

_____

_____

_____

_____

_____

_____

_____

A grid is a tool used to mark sample areas and survey biodiversity. The species within the grid are counted.

15. Describe a design problem that is addressed by the rooftop garden on the building shown in the photo.

_____

_____

_____

_____

_____

_____

_____

_____

The plants on this rooftop are part of a solution to minimize the impact that concrete, asphalt, roof tiles, and other non-absorbent surfaces have on the surrounding environment.

16. Write either a + or a − sign to identify positive or negative impacts on biodiversity.

_____ planting native plants that support native pollinators

_____ collecting rainwater to reuse for irrigation

_____ building a "rain garden" to promote filtering of runoff after rainfall

_____ constructing a road that divides habitat that was once connected

_____ clearing of land to build new buildings

Continue Your Exploration

Name: _____   Date: _____

Check out the path below or go online to choose one of the other paths shown.

| Careers in Science | • You Are an Ecosystem
• Hands-On Labs ✋
• Propose Your Own Path | Go online to choose one of these other paths. |

Restoration Ecologist

Restoration ecology is a field that focuses on restoring freshwater, marine, and land ecosystems that have been damaged by human activity. Restoration ecologists help design solutions to problems facing ecosystems. These solutions help preserve biodiversity. Restoration ecologists may provide assistance to government agencies and to businesses. Some jobs restoration ecologists might do include:

- controlling and removing invasive species
- helping farmers to use sustainable farming practices
- working to improve habitats for specific species
- planning and developing practices for soil or land conservation
- planning and implementing the restoration of ocean, lake, or stream shorelines

Restoration ecologists may work alone or with others, in the field or in an office. They often collect data in the field and return to an office or laboratory to analyze the data. Then they develop a solution to the biodiversity problem. They may use mapping and computer modeling to help in developing these solutions. Other science disciplines use similar methods and equipment to obtain and evaluate evidence. Accurately collecting and analyzing evidence and applying conclusions in a valid manner is the nature of science.

This restoration ecologist is collecting data to study the change in plant communities at a nature reserve in southern England.

Continue Your Exploration

This landfill in New York was in operation for many decades.

Through restoration and engineering efforts, the landfill is being transformed into a park that includes wildlife habitats.

1. An organization wants to restore an area's ecosystem to attract bird species that used to live there. How might a restoration ecologist help them?

2. Look at the photos of the landfill area and its restoration. Describe at least two ways that changes to living and nonliving components of the ecosystem have positively affected the biodiversity of the area.

3. What types of evidence might help determine whether the restored ecosystem has high biodiversity?

4. **Collaborate** With a group, outline a restoration project in an area in your community. Suppose that you and your classmates are the restoration ecologists planning and carrying out the work. Develop a short presentation of your proposal. Include an explanation for how the project would positively affect biodiversity in the area.

Can You Explain It?

Name: _____   Date: _____

What factors might influence how this ecosystem would recover from such a large and sudden flood?

before flood

during flood

EVIDENCE NOTEBOOK

Refer to the notes in your Evidence Notebook to help you construct an explanation for how this ecosystem might have recovered from such a huge and sudden disturbance.

1. State your claim. Make sure your claim fully explains what might influence how this ecosystem would recover from the flood.

2. Summarize the evidence you have gathered to support your claim and explain your reasoning.

Checkpoints

Answer the following questions to check your understanding of the lesson.

Use the photo to answer Question 3.

3. What can you tell about this population of king penguins and their icy South Sandwich Islands ecosystem from the photo? Choose all that apply.

    A. There is low genetic diversity in this population of king penguins.

    B. It is likely to be one of the largest bird populations in the ecosystem.

    C. Not a lot of species diversity can be seen in this photo.

    D. A lot of species diversity is shown in this photo.

4. An ecosystem with high / low biodiversity is better able to recover from a disturbance because the more biodiverse an ecosystem is, the more / less likely it is that some organisms will survive and continue to grow.

Use the photo to answer Question 5.

5. This photo shows restoration efforts at a former open-pit mine. How will the restoration of this land most likely affect populations of organisms in the surrounding area?

    A. Biodiversity will likely increase.

    B. Population sizes will likely decrease.

    C. Stability will likely decrease.

    D. Disturbances will likely increase.

6. In order to make crop growing more economical, crops such as wheat, corn, and potatoes are often grown on large areas of land where all other plants have been removed. Why can this type of planting style make crops more prone to outbreaks of disease?

    A. The high species diversity associated with croplands leads to poor crop health.

    B. Biodiversity of the cultivated land where the crops grow is very low.

    C. Genetic diversity in crops is typically high, leading to more disease outbreaks.

    D. All ecosystems managed by humans have low biodiversity and poor health.

Interactive Review

Complete this section to review the main concepts of the lesson.

Biodiversity refers to the variety of life that is a part of Earth's ecosystems. Biodiversity can be studied at the ecosystem, species, and genetic level.

A. Explain why it is important to consider all three levels of biodiversity rather than just one.

An *ecosystem disturbance* is a temporary change in environmental conditions that causes a change in an ecosystem. The health of an ecosystem can be defined by its ability to recover or remain stable when a disturbance occurs.

B. What evidence is used as an indicator of ecosystem health? Explain your answer.

Humans, just like other organisms, need healthy ecosystems in which to survive, but many human activities have negative effects on ecosystems and their biodiversity.

C. Describe how humans can influence biodiversity by using specific examples.

Ecosystems Can Stabilize in Response to Change

Bare rock is exposed for the first time in thousands of years after a glacier retreats from Aialik Bay in Kenai Fjords National Park, Alaska.

Explore First

Thinking About Changes Think of your school as an ecosystem. In groups, brainstorm ways the school could change suddenly and ways it could change gradually. Discuss how each type of change would affect the students, teachers, and staff at the school.

Go online to view the digital version of the Hands-On Lab for this lesson and to download additional lab resources.

CAN YOU EXPLAIN IT?

How would the arrival of a swarm of millions of desert locusts affect an ecosystem?

Desert locusts look and act a lot like grasshoppers, although they are larger. They normally eat plants and live alone. However, certain changes in environmental conditions, such as a drought, can cause them to come together in swarms to travel long distances to find food.

1. Why might a drought cause normally solitary desert locusts to change their behavior and swarm?

2. How might swarming locusts affect planted crops? How might the swarms affect local populations of humans and insect-eating birds?

EVIDENCE NOTEBOOK As you explore the lesson, gather evidence to help explain how an insect swarm would affect an ecosystem.

Describing Changes in Ecosystems

Yikes! You lift up a rotting log from a forest floor and several insects dash away from it. You disturbed their ecosystem! An *ecosystem* is a natural system in which organisms interact with the living and nonliving parts of their environment.

Insects are not the only living things in a forest floor ecosystem. You might also observe spiders, fungi, snails, mosses, worms, or a toad. Vines, ferns, and other plants might also grow on the forest floor. All of these living organisms depend on each other and the nonliving parts of the ecosystem. The nonliving parts include rocks, nutrients, air, and water. The log on the forest floor is not alive, but it supports lots of life. Some living things break down the log's cells for food. This decomposition releases nutrients from the log back into the soil. In this way, energy and matter cycle between the living and nonliving parts of an ecosystem.

Explore Online

Forest Floor Ecosystem

Ecosystems, even tiny ones, contain living and nonliving parts that interact. Plants take in minerals from the soil and carbon dioxide from the air. Snails eat plants. They also eat soil to get calcium for their shells.

3. A system input is any energy, matter, or information that enters a system. Which factors would be inputs of a forest floor ecosystem? Select the correct answers.

   A. soil

   B. sunlight

   C. rain

   D. trees

4. **Discuss** How do you think a decrease in one of these inputs would affect the forest floor ecosystem?

Ecosystems Change Over Time

Ecosystems are dynamic, which means their characteristics can change over time. Even healthy ecosystems with high biodiversity change a bit every day. In every ecosystem, organisms are born, some die, and all living things respond to changes. Ecosystems with high biodiversity can recover from changes more easily than those with lower biodiversity can. Some changes, such as the seasons, are gradual. Other changes, such as a storm or a flood, are sudden.

Seasonal Changes

spring   summer   fall   winter

Changes in temperature, precipitation and sunlight occur during the seasons. They cause changes in ecosystems. This tree goes from budding new leaves in spring to full bloom in summer. Then it loses its leaves in the fall and is inactive through the winter.

5. Classify each statement as a change to a living factor or a change to a nonliving factor.

Change	Change to Living Factor	Change to Nonliving Factor
Birds migrate in fall.		
Ice that covers lakes melts in spring.		
Temperature increases in summer.		
Leaves fall from trees in fall.		
Seeds sprout in spring.		
Water in soil freezes in winter.		

6. Some bird populations that live in the Northern Hemisphere migrate to warmer climates for the winter. Identify reasons birds might respond this way to a seasonal change in their habitat.

Gradual Changes

Gradual changes are going on all the time in every ecosystem. For example, ponds and lakes undergo an aging process that involves gradual changes over hundreds of years. Sediment builds up in a body of water, eventually changing it into land. Sediment buildup also leads to natural *eutrophication*. During this process, nutrients from plants and rock minerals dissolve in the water. The nutrients boost growth of plants and algae. When the plants and algae die, they decompose. Decomposition requires oxygen, so over time, the water becomes depleted of oxygen.

As these changes occur, the pond ecosystem also changes. Fish, amphibian, and insect populations will die out or move to a different pond. Eventually, all populations living in the pond ecosystem will be affected by the change. Gradual changes also take place as glaciers melt, logs rot, and climates change. Even a relatively small increase in temperatures can have a widespread effect on ecosystems.

Over a long period of time, this pond filled up with sediment and changed into a meadow.

sediment builds up

7. The effects of the change to the pond will most likely be
   short term / long term as the pond ecosystem
   changes to a meadow. The living and nonliving parts of the
   ecosystems will change / stay the same.

Sudden Changes

Forest fires, tornadoes, volcanic eruptions, and floods can all cause sudden changes to an ecosystem. For example, if a river floods, its banks may overflow. The river banks may erode and cause the river water to become too muddy or too fast flowing for fish and other river organisms to survive. Living things that depend on fish for food may be negatively affected because their food source is gone.

Sudden changes happen quickly and can kill or remove several populations of organisms from an ecosystem at once. Similarly to a slow change, sudden changes can be local or widespread. An event that causes changes to the living or nonliving parts of an ecosystem is called a **disturbance**. Some disturbances are natural processes. Other disturbances are caused by humans when they damage or remove parts of an ecosystem.

In just minutes, a tornado causes a sudden ecosystem change. Powerful winds rip trees and other plants from the soil and may kill or displace many animals.

8. The photos show two different ecosystems after sudden changes. Compare and contrast these two changes. Write your observations in the space provided.

This forest fire caused several changes in the forest habitat.

Ash, gases, and lava from a volcanic eruption affect the area around the volcano.

9. What organisms or populations do you think might be directly or indirectly affected by each of these sudden changes?

Effects of Changes in Ecosystems

Since each part of an ecosystem is interconnected, a change to any part can affect populations in the larger ecosystem. Consider a population that is removed from an ecosystem for some reason. Another species in the same ecosystem may fill the "gap" left by the missing species. Or the species might not be replaced at all.

Small changes in one part of an ecosystem can lead to large changes in other parts of the ecosystem. For example, suppose a disease killed one species of bee in an ecosystem. Bees are important pollinators. In ecosystems with more than one bee species, the remaining species might expand when one dies off. But if there is only one bee species in the area and it dies off, there would be fewer pollinators in the ecosystem. Insect-pollinated plants might not be able to reproduce, which would mean there would be less food for animals that eat seeds, fruit, or vegetables from these plants. Over time, the change in the bee species would affect many populations.

EVIDENCE NOTEBOOK

10. Think about the swarm of locusts you saw at the beginning of the lesson. Is the swarm a change to a living or a nonliving ecosystem component? Is the change gradual or sudden? Record your evidence.

Ecosystems Recover from Change

After a disturbance, an ecosystem begins to recover. **Succession** is the process of recovery and change that happens after a disturbance. Sometimes the original community may grow back. Other times the changes to an ecosystem are so severe that populations that once lived there die out or do not return. Then, succession begins when certain organisms, called *pioneer species*, begin to grow. For example, after a glacier retreats, only bare rock remains. Pioneer species such as lichens can grow on rock and help to form soil. Over time, other plants and animals return. The ecosystem becomes more complex when it is able to support more types of organisms. Biodiversity gradually increases, and the ecosystem eventually stabilizes. The variety of species and number of individuals in a population tend to increase with time after a disturbance.

Language SmArts

Analyze Rate of Environmental Change

Artificial eutrophication results from pollution and occurs much faster than natural eutrophication. In artificial eutrophication, runoff from farms, mines, or household waste, adds large amounts of nutrients such as phosphorus and nitrogen to a body of water. The nutrients support large algal blooms—population explosions of algae—in the water. As the algae die and decompose, oxygen is depleted from the water. The algae may also produce toxins that kill other living things, such as fish and amphibians. More oxygen is used as their bodies decay. As a result, organisms may not be able to live in the water.

Excess nutrients from fertilizer runoff caused a toxic bloom of cyanobacteria in the Copco Reservoir in California.

11. Compared to natural eutrophication, nutrient pollution is a relatively sudden / gradual change to the lake ecosystem. Populations of birds in the area that feed on fish from the lake would likely stay / move away. As a result of eutrophication, the biodiversity of the lake ecosystem would likely increase / decrease.

12. If artificial eutrophication continues, what changes do you think will occur in the ecosystem and in this area? Use evidence to explain your reasoning.

_____

_____

_____

_____

_____

Predicting Changes to Populations

An ecosystem disturbance can be caused by the introduction of a nonnative species, such as the introduction of eastern gray squirrels to Europe. Gray squirrels are native to the eastern United States. They were introduced to several locations in the United Kingdom and Ireland between 1876 and 1929. The species quickly adapted to their new forest ecosystems. The total population of gray squirrels in Europe has increased greatly since their introduction.

Red squirrels are native to Europe and northern Asia. Gray squirrels are larger and more aggressive than red squirrels. They eat a larger variety of foods. They also have fewer predators than red squirrels do. As a result, gray squirrels took over much of the red squirrels' resources and the red squirrel population decreased across Europe.

The eastern gray squirrel has quite a varied diet. It eats nuts, flowers, fruits, seeds, tree bark, fungi, frogs, eggs, and bird hatchlings.

Eurasian red squirrels prefer to eat the seeds of trees, but will also eat berries, young plant shoots, and bird eggs.

13. Compare and contrast potential effects of two disturbances on a native population of red squirrels—a storm and the introduction of nonnative gray squirrels. Fill in the Venn diagram using the statements.

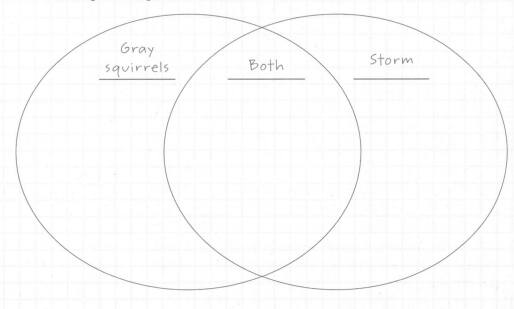

Gray squirrels

Both

Storm

WORD BANK
- competes for resources
- decreases available food
- reduces available living space
- causes sudden change
- introduces disease

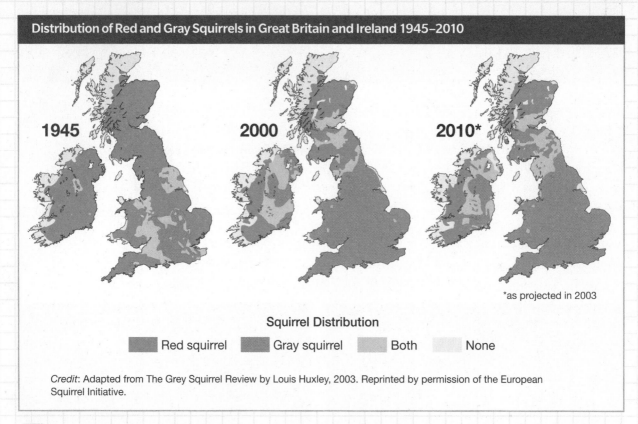

Distribution of Red and Gray Squirrels in Great Britain and Ireland 1945–2010

1945 2000 2010*

*as projected in 2003

Squirrel Distribution

Red squirrel   Gray squirrel   Both   None

Credit: Adapted from The Grey Squirrel Review by Louis Huxley, 2003. Reprinted by permission of the European Squirrel Initiative.

14. Language SmArts In your own words, describe the changes in the distribution of red and gray squirrels from 1945 to 2010.

The introduction of gray squirrels into Europe had a negative impact on populations of red squirrels. Scientists also identified that gray squirrels negatively affected populations of songbirds, and likely spread the disease squirrel pox to red squirrels. Gray squirrels also eat the bark from trees in winter, causing the trees to be more prone to disease. However, the presence of gray squirrels helped another species— pine martens—to rebound from the point of extinction.

Scientists determined that gray squirrels likely had a positive effect on the populations of pine martens. Pine martens are weasel-like predators of squirrels. Pine martens were hunted to near extinction in the United Kingdom and Ireland in the early 20th century. Farmers and landowners considered them pests because they ate chickens and young lambs. Since pine martens became a protected species in the 1980s, their numbers have grown. Researchers noted that pine martens prefer eating gray squirrels to red squirrels. Gray squirrels are larger, slower, and spend more time on the ground, which means that pine martens can catch gray squirrels more easily. With more food, pine marten populations in Ireland and Scotland have increased, and the rate of gray squirrel population growth has decreased.

Effects of Ecosystem Changes on Populations

Ecosystem components are connected, so changes to living and nonliving parts can affect populations. The removal of a species, the decrease of a food source, or a change in temperature can cause large changes in the other parts of the ecosystems. For example, several years of increased average winter temperatures can cause seeds to germinate earlier and change the behavior of migrating animals.

A change may displace or kill individuals and populations. A large portion of a population may move because of a disturbance, such as a flood, and not return. If this happens, there may not be enough individuals to sustain the population in that area over time, and the local population could die out.

Bangladesh, a country in South Asia, is prone to flooding because it is low-lying and has a long coastline. The frequent flooding affects human, animal, and plant populations.

Do the Math

Identify Factors That Change Populations

Before the arrival of European settlers in North America, about 46% of the land was forested. Early settlers spoke of towering white pine trees. White pines were one of the many native species that were heavily harvested for building ship masts, wagons, fences, and furniture. Clearing of old-growth forests for agriculture and commercial purposes hit its highest rate in the mid-1800s and continued until the mid-1920s.

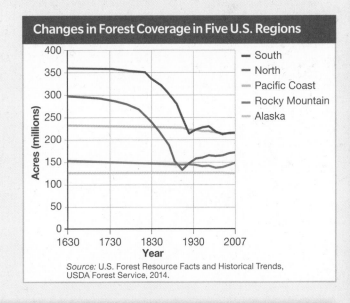

Changes in Forest Coverage in Five U.S. Regions

— South
— North
— Pacific Coast
— Rocky Mountain
— Alaska

Source: U.S. Forest Resource Facts and Historical Trends, USDA Forest Service, 2014.

15. What information about forest coverage does the graph tell you?

16. The Carolina parakeet once lived in large flocks in old-growth forests in the eastern and southeastern United States. Their extinction has been linked to the removal of old-growth forests. Based on the graph, when do you think Carolina parakeet populations decreased the most? Give a reason for your answer.

Hands-On Lab
Identify Factors That Influence a Population Change

Simulate population changes in a pack of wolves and identify specific changes that affect this population.

Procedure

STEP 1 Place eight popcorn kernels on the table. Two kernels represent adult wolves, the other six represent a litter of pups.

STEP 2 Follow the game play key that is shown below. The game play key will allow you to model ecosystem changes that affect a wolf population by throwing the dice. Some of the changes to the ecosystem are natural events and some are caused by humans.

If you roll . . .	You . . .	Reason
Double 2s, 3s, 4s, or 5s	Subtract 3	Nursing female ingests rat poison; pups die
2	Divide by 2 (round down)	Disease introduced by stray dogs; half the pack dies
3	Subtract 4	Drought occurs, causing food shortage for prey
4 (1+3)	Subtract 1	One wolf dies of natural causes
5	Subtract 2	A harmful pollutant builds up in the tissues of rabbits; wolves eat the rabbits and get poisoned
6 (2+4 or 1+5) or 7	Make no changes	Rains arrive; pack lives well for six months
8 (2+6 or 3+5)	Subtract 1	One pup dies of natural causes
9 or 11	Make no changes	Elk population remains high due to plentiful plant growth; wolves live well for six months
10 (4+6)	Subtract 1	Habitat size decreases due to development; male killed in territorial dispute with another wolf pack
12	Add 1	New, mature wolf joins pack

STEP 3 On a separate sheet of paper, make a table similar to the one below. The table should record the results of 15 years of data.

Year	Last year's total	Add a litter (+6)	First 6 months		Second 6 months		Pack subtotal	Subtract matured pups?	Total pack for year
			Reason	Effect on pack	Reason	Effect on pack			
1	2	+6						no	
2								no	
3									

© Houghton Mifflin Harcourt Publishing Company

STEP 4 Roll the dice to represent the passage of six months. Use the total number on the dice to determine what happens to your pack, according to the game play key. Then fill in the information in your data table. As you record data, also record the reason for the population change in the *Reason* column. Adjust the number of kernels that represent your wolf pack.

STEP 5 Repeat Step 4 for the second six months of the year. Count the number of wolves in your pack and fill in the rest of Year 1 in the data table.

STEP 6 Reproduction: After Year 1, adjust the number of kernels to add six pups at the beginning of each year unless a food shortage occurred the previous year.

STEP 7 Maturation: When the pack gets too large, the mature pups leave. Subtract six wolves if your pack has more than nine wolves. Adjust the number of kernels you have accordingly. Record the pack total in the last column of the table.

STEP 8 Repeat Steps 4–7 until you complete 15 years of play or until your pack dies out, whichever comes first.

Analysis

STEP 9 What patterns did you notice in the types of ecosystem changes that affected your wolf pack? Did a relatively small change have a larger impact on the wolf population? Explain your answer.

STEP 10 How might a change to a wolf pack affect other populations, such as the elk or bison that the wolves feed on?

STEP 11 Does evidence from your model suggest that many different types of changes correlate with changes in the wolf population? Explain your answer.

EVIDENCE NOTEBOOK

17. Desert locusts are plant eaters and are eaten by animals such as snakes, birds, and small mammals. What effects might the swarm of locusts have on other populations in an ecosystem? Record your evidence.

Populations That Depend on Disturbance

In the early 1900s, a major goal of the United States Forest Service was to stop forest fires. One reason for this effort was to prevent the destruction of timber resources. However, around the 1960s, scientists began to recognize that the fires were important to the stability of forest ecosystems. They realized that a forest ecosystem becomes unhealthy if fires do not occur periodically. Scientists observed that if every fire is prevented, trees become overcrowded and dead plant material builds up on the forest floor. Today, scientists know that fires add nutrients to soil. Fires clear the forest floor, providing space for seedlings. They can also thin out the tree canopy, which allows more sunlight to reach the forest floor. Saplings and other plants can then grow.

Sequoias are adapted to survive forest fires. The trees depend on fires to reduce competition from other trees that may crowd out their germinating seedlings.

Some populations depend on fires. For example, populations of sequoias, a type of redwood tree, depend on forest fires to reproduce. They need low-intensity fires to release seeds from their cones. Forest fires also reduce competition from other species.

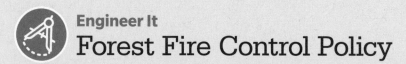

Engineer It
Forest Fire Control Policy

Fire suppression is the process of preventing or putting out forest fires. It was a tool commonly used in the past to prevent forest fires. In the late 1890s, conservationists identified forest fires as a major threat to the U.S. economy because they destroyed the supply of timber. In 1910, the U.S. government began a policy of total fire suppression. The policy involved preventing fires and also putting out a fire as quickly as possible once one started. Later, researchers observed that the fire suppression policy had unintended effects on forest ecosystems. Populations of plants that depended on fires to complete their life cycles were negatively affected and forest ecosystems were changing. Such observations led to a policy change in the 1970s. Today, the U.S. Forest Service manages and controls, rather than totally extinguishes, forest fires.

18. Imagine you are a forest ranger. Define the engineering design problem you face in developing a solution to allow the fire-dependent plants in the forest you manage to carry out their life cycle. You want to minimize fire hazards for people who visit and live near the forest. You also need to be mindful of air pollution laws. List at least three criteria and three constraints that would influence your solution.

_____

_____

_____

_____

_____

Continue Your Exploration

Name: _____   **Date:** _____

Check out the path below or go online to choose one of the other paths shown.

People in Science

- Ecological Succession
- Cockroaches vs. Pandas
- Hands-On Labs 🖐
- Propose Your Own Path

Go online to choose one of these other paths.

Rodolfo Dirzo, Terrestrial Ecologist

Rodolfo Dirzo grew up in Morelos in southern Mexico. As a boy, he loved to explore the area's remaining patches of dry tropical forests. Dirzo would capture glowing insects and place them in a plastic bag to make a lantern so that he could continue his explorations after dark. This early interest in the natural world led Dirzo to pursue a degree at the local university, where he studied how deforestation impacts the quality and availability of water in southern Mexico. He later earned a doctorate from the University of Wales, where he studied plant and animal interactions. Dirzo's current research examines what happens to ecosystems when animal populations decrease or disappear because of human activity. His research takes him to savannas in east Africa, tropical forests in Mexico, and the oak woodlands of northern California, to name a few.

Rodolfo Dirzo with an elephant in Kenya, where he has studied what happens when large plant-eating animals are removed from ecosystems.

Oak Woodland Regeneration

Oak woodlands are ecosystems dominated by oak trees. Dirzo and his team have found that the number of young oaks in northern California oak woodlands is very limited. Young oaks replace mature oaks in a cycle of regeneration for the woodlands, so the low number of young oak trees may mean that the oak woodlands are unable to regenerate in the future.

Bears and cougars were once top predators in the oak woodland ecosystem. Their numbers have decreased due to hunting and habitat destruction. As these predators decline, the populations of their prey may increase, including deer. Deer graze on oak seedlings, so an increase in the deer population can lead to overgrazing of oak seedlings, reducing the numbers of young oaks. Dirzo hypothesizes that the loss of top predators may also lead to a reshaping of plant communities due to an increase in populations of plant-eating animals and smaller prey animals.

Continue Your Exploration

Oak woodlands like this one provide important ecosystem services, such as water filtration and helping to prevent erosion and mudslides. They are also rich in biodiversity.

1. Develop a diagram that models how a change in the population of a top predator in the oak woodlands could affect regeneration of the oaks.

2. Imagine you have collected data showing that the number of young oaks in the woodlands has decreased as the deer population has increased. Does this finding provide evidence of a causal relationship or of a correlation? Explain your answer.

3. How might cattle grazing of the woodlands impact oak tree regeneration? Explain your reasoning.

4. **Collaborate** Dirzo uses the term defaunation to describe the impact humans have on animal populations. *Deforestation* refers to destruction of trees and plant life due to human activity. *Fauna* refers to animal life. Using these clues, work with a partner to develop a definition for *defaunation*. How might defaunation affect society? Share an example of defaunation and its effects with the class.

Can You Explain It?

Name: _____   Date: _____

How would the arrival of a swarm of millions of desert locusts affect an ecosystem?

EVIDENCE NOTEBOOK

Refer to the notes in your Evidence Notebook to help you construct an explanation for how a swarm of locusts can affect an ecosystem.

1. State your claim. Make sure your claim fully explains how this disturbance could affect the ecosystem.

2. Summarize the evidence you have gathered to support your claim and explain your reasoning.

Checkpoints

Answer the following questions to check your understanding of the lesson.

Use the photo to answer Questions 3 and 4.

3. A lahar is a mudflow caused by a volcanic eruption. Lahars destroy most things in their paths as they rush downhill, burying parts of the landscape. Which statement best describes a lahar and the populations it affects?

   A. It is sudden and affects few populations.

   B. It is sudden and affects most populations.

   C. It is gradual and affects only animal populations.

   D. It is sudden and affects only plant populations.

a lahar

4. In 1980, Mt. St. Helens erupted. The resulting lahar flowed over a wide area of the Cascade Mountains. Which of these statements best describes the effect of the volcanic eruption? Select all that apply.

   A. It affected the living and nonliving components of the ecosystem.

   B. It removed populations of mammals from the mountainside.

   C. It led to succession on the mountainside.

   D. It affected only nonliving components of the ecosystem.

Use the map to answer Questions 5 and 6.

5. Near the coasts there has been loss only / loss and gain / gain only of forests. In north-central Washington and British Columbia, there are large patches of forest loss / forest gain.

6. Historically, the Pacific Northwest region experienced much less deforestation than other regions of the United States. Therefore, populations of organisms living in Pacific Northwest forest ecosystems are likely to have experienced relatively few / many changes to their environment. Changes in the populations of tree species would likely affect / not affect other populations living in the forest.

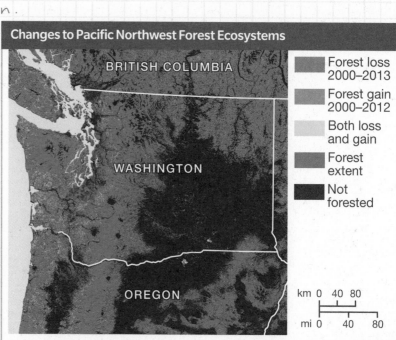

Changes to Pacific Northwest Forest Ecosystems

BRITISH COLUMBIA

WASHINGTON

OREGON

Forest loss 2000–2013
Forest gain 2000–2012
Both loss and gain
Forest extent
Not forested

km 0 40 80
mi 0 40 80

Credit: Adapted from Global Forest Change, University of Maryland, Department of Geographical Sciences. Reprinted by permission of M.C. Hansen.

Interactive Review

Complete this section to review the main concepts of the lesson.

Ecosystems contain populations of living organisms as well as nonliving things.
Ecosystem disturbances change habitats in different ways .

A. How do sudden and gradual disturbances each affect ecosystems?

Different types of disturbances have different effects on populations. A change in one
part of an ecosystem can affect many populations.

B. Use examples to explain how changes to both living and nonliving parts of an ecosystem can affect individuals and populations.

iStock/Getty Images Plus/Getty Images; (b) ©maislam/Fotolia

Maintaining Biodiversity and Ecosystem Services

These solar-powered Supertrees and elevated walkways are in Singapore's Gardens by the Bay. They are inspiring examples of how human creativity can preserve biodiversity.

Explore First

Choosing Building Materials Imagine you are tasked with building a foot bridge across a stream for hikers in a forest. The stream sometimes floods, so the bridge must be made of a material that is not harmed by water and will not become slippery. What material would you build the bridge out of, and why?

Go online to view the digital version of the Hands-On Lab for this lesson and to download additional lab resources.

CAN YOU EXPLAIN IT?

How can we develop a solution to biodiversity loss in the Everglades without shutting humans out of this endangered ecosystem?

The manatee is just one of the endangered species living in Florida's Everglades, a large wetland ecosystem. Habitat loss and collisions with watercraft are two major threats to manatees.

1. Which design solutions protect biodiversity and consider human needs? Select all that apply.

   A. installing walkways that leave wildlife undisturbed

   B. building houses on a filled-in wetland

   C. using water from lakes to supply farmland

   D. creating no-fishing zones

2. What ideas do you have for how boaters might enjoy the wetlands of Florida's Everglades without harming manatee habitats?

 EVIDENCE NOTEBOOK As you explore this lesson, gather evidence to help you explain how to develop a solution to biodiversity loss in the Everglades.

Evaluating Biodiversity Loss

As the sun rises on a coastal mangrove forest, all seems quiet and still. But upon closer observation, the forest is full of activity. The forest's network of branches and roots provides enough food for a diverse community of organisms. The underwater roots are a perfect nursery for many fish. The forest is also home to native and migratory birds.

Mangrove forests are full of life. The dense tangle of roots props the trees above high tides.

3. A fishing boat by a mangrove forest spills a chemical that is deadly to aquatic plants. What changes might happen as a result? Select all that apply.

   A. Many trees become poisoned and die.

   B. Fish eggs fail due to loss of nursery habitat.

   C. Mangrove shrimp become unsafe for humans to eat.

   D. Erosion from the loss of trees causes decreased water quality.

Humans Rely on Healthy Ecosystems

Humans depend on resources provided by healthy ecosystems. For example, fish breed in mangrove forests. Therefore, the forests provide food and jobs for people who live nearby. The mangroves' dense roots trap sediments and filter out impurities. So, the forests also provide clean water. Mangrove forests even help protect houses near the shore. They block damaging storm winds, reduce soil erosion, and prevent flooding.

The health of an ecosystem, such as a mangrove forest, can be defined by how well it can recover from disturbances. The higher the biodiversity level within an ecosystem, the healthier it is. However, different ecosystems can differ in their biodiversity and still be thought of as "healthy." For example, an arctic ecosystem naturally has far less biodiversity than a coral reef ecosystem does. It is when the biodiversity of an ecosystem decreases from its "healthiest" level that problems can happen. As an ecosystem loses its biodiversity, natural resources become less available. Services provided by ecosystems with lowered biodiversity may also become less reliable.

4. Scientists and engineers study ways to help coral reefs recover from damage by boats or pollution. How does this show that science and technology can have positive and negative effects on biodiversity?

Coral reefs have stunning biodiversity. However, they recover very slowly from disturbances because corals grow slowly.

Ecosystems Provide Natural Resources

Living and nonliving parts of an ecosystem provide humans with natural resources. A *natural resource* is any natural material that is used by humans. Humans rely on ecosystems for natural resources such as fresh water, food, medicines, energy, clothing, and building materials.

For example, few areas on Earth have more natural resources than the Amazon rain forest. The Amazon River flows more than 6,920 kilometers (4,300 miles) across Peru and Brazil to the Atlantic Ocean. It provides water for drinking, transportation, and agriculture. It supports more than 2,500 species of fish and thousands of species on land. Chemical compounds in rainforest plants are used as medicines. Plants growing in the forests are an important source of atmospheric oxygen. However, there are many threats to the health of the Amazon rain forest. Trees are cleared and rivers are dammed to generate power. The health of any ecosystem affects the health of communities and the supply of resources to them.

Natural Resources Provided by Ecosystems

Humans use or change Earth's many resources to live comfortably.

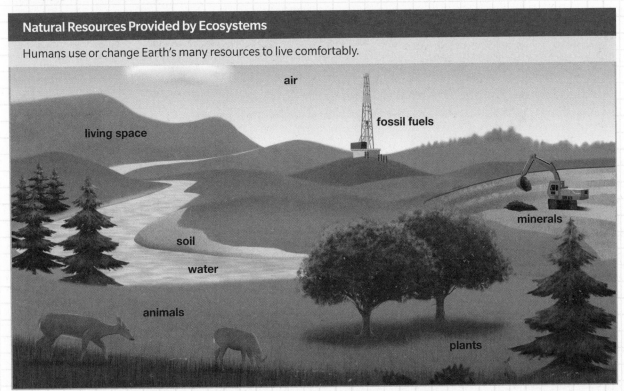

5. Match each product with the natural resource used to make it.

concrete	fossil fuels
timber for housing	plants
gasoline	minerals

6. How does the availability of natural resources depend on ecosystem health? Use an example to explain.

Ecosystems Provide Services

Matter cycles and energy flows through the living and nonliving parts of ecosystems by natural processes. Humans benefit from many of these natural processes. An **ecosystem service** is any ecosystem function that provides benefits to humans. The benefits can be direct or indirect, small or large. Water purification, nutrient recycling, and climate regulation are ecosystem services. Pollination and pest and disease control are also important services.

Analyze Threats to Five Ecosystem Services

7. What environmental changes might threaten each of these ecosystem services? Include those caused by human activities.

Ecosystem Service	Potential Threats
Water filtration: Filtration by soil, rock, and plants provides clean water. Humans use this water for drinking, industry, and recreation. Filtration helps prevent microbe-related illness and the nutrient poisoning of lakes from farmland runoff.	
Decomposition: Soil microbes break down dead matter and nutrients are released into the ecosystem. This improves soil quality and decreases the need for artificial fertilizers.	
Pollination: Many plants must be pollinated by animals to produce fruit and seeds. Such plants include over 150 food crops in the United States. Insects and birds are pollinators. They need enough undisturbed nesting sites to live and reproduce.	
Erosion control: The extensive root systems of native plants and trees anchor soils. Thus, they prevent erosion and reduce the effects of floods. Root systems of crops are not as extensive. Therefore, they do not provide the same benefit.	
Climate regulation: Tiny marine phytoplankton are producers in marine ecosystems. They carry out more than half of all photosynthesis on Earth. They help maintain levels of oxygen and carbon dioxide in the air and in the oceans.	

8. **Discuss** What ecosystem services do you depend on every day? Brainstorm ways your life would be different if you did not have these services where you live.

Loss of Biodiversity Affects Ecosystem Health

When biodiversity declines in an ecosystem, there are fewer natural resources and services to support the remaining organisms. The ecosystem is no longer as healthy, or stable, as before. Biodiversity can decline due to environmental changes, such as a drought. It can also be reduced by human activities, such as urban development and agriculture.

One example of biodiversity loss involves coffee plantations. Coffee plants grow well in the tropical, species-rich areas of the world. There are two main methods of farming coffee. Traditionally, the shrub-like coffee plants are grown in shade. They are planted among existing trees. Leaving the trees standing protects the habitat of birds. The birds eat pests that might damage the crop. The trees drop leaves that cover the ground and help prevent weed growth. Decomposition of the leaves also increases nutrient cycling.

Shade-grown coffee plantations protect existing species diversity. The coffee plants produce beans for about 30 years.

As demand for coffee grows, the expansion of coffee plantations into deforested areas is rising. Deforestation removes all plant species from an area. Sun-grown coffee does not get the benefits provided by trees, so fertilization is necessary. Cutting down trees also increases erosion and fertilizer runoff into nearby streams and lakes. Sun-grown coffee plants must also be replaced more often than shade-grown plants. Replacing plants is an added cost for farmers.

Humans make choices about how they impact ecosystem health when they get natural resources. Scientists and engineers play an important role in these choices. They research and design ways to maintain biodiversity and ecosystem stability.

Coffee plants grown in the sun produce more beans per acre. But bean quality and volume decrease after about 15 years.

9. In comparison to sun-grown coffee, shade-grown coffee needs more / less fertilization and more / less pesticide treatment. Shade-grown coffee plantations are more / less affected by erosion than sun-grown plantations. For these reasons, coffee grown in the shade / sun helps maintain biodiversity and ecosystem health.

Do the Math
Compare Costs and Benefits of Shade-Grown Coffee

10. What is the yearly profit from coffee beans grown in a shade-grown plot and a sun-grown plot?

11. Consider the lifespan of the coffee plants. What is the total profit over the lifespan of coffee plants in a sun-grown plot? What is the total profit over the lifespan of plants in a shade-grown plot? What are some other costs and benefits of each type of plot?

Variable measured	Sun-grown coffee	Shade-grown coffee
Coffee beans produced per plot, per year	1,600 kg	550 kg
Diseased coffee plants per plot, per year	5	<1
Lifespan of plants	15 years	30 years
Profit per kilogram of coffee produced	$2.00	$2.50*
(*Shade-grown coffee sells at a higher price when certified as "bird friendly.")		

Causes of Biodiversity Loss

Humans love to expand and explore. This leads to important cultural progress, but it also can cause long-term changes to ecosystems. Human activities can cause **habitat destruction**, the changing or loss of a natural ecosystem. Habitat destruction removes living space and resources needed by organisms.

Most negative impacts on ecosystems are the result of urbanization, farming, industry, or energy production. As the human population grows, resource use also increases. For example, sharks are threatened by overfishing due to demand for their fins and meat. Shark fin soup is a traditional dish in some cultures. Sharks may also be trapped by fishing nets used to catch other species. As top predators, sharks help maintain biodiversity by controlling the balance of other fish populations. Without proper planning, fishermen may destroy fish populations that provide their source of income. Human activities are the largest threat to biodiversity. Therefore, solutions need to involve changes to these activities.

Humans kill about 100 million sharks every year. To save them, fisheries and consumers of shark products need to be part of the solution.

EVIDENCE NOTEBOOK

12. Human activities have destroyed miles of Everglade wetlands for development. How do these changes affect ecosystem health and nearby human communities? Record your evidence.

13. Changes in the health of one population can cause a cascade of effects in other populations. Consider the decline of shark populations. Sharks prey on sea turtles, which eat plants. Number the phrases to complete the cause-and-effect chain.

_____ seagrasses overgrazed

_____ loss of sharks

_____ fish nurseries destroyed

_____ sea turtles increase

Language SmArts
Evaluate Agricultural Practices

Trees and other plants may be clear-cut to make room for crops farmers grow. This displaces native species and reduces biodiversity in the ecosystem. Water used to irrigate crops removes nutrients from the soil. The soil quality declines, and the removal of vegetation causes it to erode more easily. It travels to new locations without adding nutrients to these areas. Fertilizers and pesticides used to maintain crops pollute air, water, and soil.

Some farming practices can reduce these negative impacts. For example, providing habitat for birds that eat insects helps reduce the need for pesticides. Alternating crop types each year helps preserve soil nutrients. Planting cover plants, such as alfalfa, reduces erosion, adds nutrients to the soil, and controls weeds.

All native plants are often removed when preparing land to grow crops. The resulting loose soil erodes easily.

14. How does the clear-cutting of trees and native plants for farming affect humans? Circle all that apply.

A. Air quality decreases as wind draws dust into the air.

B. Species diversity in the ecosystem increases.

C. Water quality decreases due to increased erosion.

D. Rainwater runoff increases, which can cause erosion.

15. Consider this claim: "Removing all native plant life on land for farming is justified because it provides more space for crops. The growing human population needs more products grown by farmers, such as food crops and meat." Do you agree or disagree? Evaluate the claim and provide evidence for your argument.

_____

_____

_____

_____

_____

Analyzing Strategies for Maintaining Biodiversity

Micronesia is an arc of more than 2,000 islands between Hawaii and the Philippines. Many of the islands are surrounded by coral reefs that are threatened by human activity. Of the 1,400 plant species on the islands, about 360 are found only on the islands. Many of these species are endangered. The islands are remote, so the people of Micronesia depend on the resources provided by the islands. Rising sea levels and human activities are depleting the islands' resources. Activities such as deforestation, overfishing, pollution, and destruction of coral reefs harm wildlife and local economies.

Conservation efforts in Micronesia are underway. They include enacting a multi-island agreement to preserve coastlines, identify coral reefs that need to be protected, and address harmful fishing practices. These efforts show that maintaining biodiversity requires collaboration among scientists, citizens, governments, and businesses.

16. Examine the coral reef photos. How does coral reef bleaching demonstrate how many small changes can weaken entire ecosystems?

Corals get their color and their food from tiny photosynthetic algae that live in the corals' tissues.

When populations of photosynthetic algae inside corals decline, the corals lose their main food source and turn white in a process called *bleaching*. The causes of bleaching include increased water temperature and pollution.

Protect Individual Species

Officials must choose where to direct limited conservation resources. Protection efforts often focus on species facing local extinction or those that most influence the success of other populations.

One cause of local extinction is overharvesting. This happens when humans reduce the population of a living resource to the point where reproduction rates are too low to restore the population. For example, Pacific bluefin tuna populations have dropped dramatically due to decades of overfishing. Most Pacific bluefin tuna caught are too young to reproduce, which leaves very few reproducing adults. The species is in danger of extinction and being considered for protection under the Endangered Species Act.

Protecting a species is also important if it is a *keystone species*. Keystone species are vital to ecosystem functioning because they affect the survival of many other species in the community. For example, sea otters are a keystone species in the North Pacific Ocean. Sea otters prey on sea urchins and other invertebrates that eat giant kelp. This helps to prevent overgrazing of kelp forests, an important marine habitat.

Two Endangered Keystone Species

Explore Online

Otters are a keystone species. Conservation efforts include protecting them from poachers, nets, and habitat loss.

Overfishing and illegal catching of bluefin tuna continue to threaten the species, despite conservation efforts.

Protect and Maintain Habitats

Most habitat destruction is the result of land clearing. However, other human activities add to the problems of habitat loss. For example, the Indiana bat must hibernate in cool, humid caves to survive winter. Rising temperatures due to climate change are decreasing the number of caves that bats can use. Also, disturbing hibernating bats can cause them to die of starvation. Some 50,000 bats can hibernate in just one cave. So, a single hiker may affect a large percentage of this endangered bat population.

Human activities can also cause **habitat fragmentation**, the division of an ecosystem into smaller areas by roads, housing communities, farms, or other development. Fragmentation makes it difficult for species to have enough space to live. Large predators, such as Florida panthers, need large land areas to hunt, find mates, and raise their young. Without enough space, these species might face local extinction.

Causes of habitat fragmentation include roads, factories, housing developments, farms, and recreation areas. Land bridges are one solution to reduce the effects of habitat fragmentation.

Hands-On Lab
Model Habitat Fragmentation

Use sheets of paper to model undisturbed and fragmented habitats and compare interior-to-edge ratios to draw conclusions about the effects of habitat fragmentation.

MATERIALS
- calculator
- ruler
- scissors
- sheets of paper (2)

Procedure and Analysis

STEP 1 Calculate and record the area of each sheet of paper by multiplying the length by the width.

STEP 2 One sheet of paper will represent an undisturbed habitat. Do not cut this paper. Model fragmentation by cutting the second sheet of paper into 5 to 10 rectangles.

STEP 3 Measure and record the perimeter of the undisturbed habitat. The perimeter is the distance around the outer edge of the paper.

STEP 4 Calculate the total perimeter of the fragmented habitat by measuring the perimeter of each piece and adding them. Record the total perimeter.

STEP 5 The perimeter of a habitat is also called the habitat's edge. Which habitat has more edge?

STEP 6 If two habitats have the same total area, is more or less edge beneficial to a species? Explain your reasoning.

STEP 7 **Do the Math** One characteristic of a habitat is its *interior-to-edge ratio*. This ratio is calculated by dividing the area of a habitat by its total perimeter. Calculate the interior-to-edge ratio for each habitat, undisturbed and fragmented.

STEP 8 *Edge effects* are the changes to populations that happen at the boundary between two ecosystems. Edge effects can occur some distance into both ecosystems. Biologists associate a large interior-to-edge ratio with fewer edge effects. Which habitat has the greatest interior-to-edge ratio? What might this mean for the species that live in each habitat?

STEP 9 On a separate sheet of paper, draw a simple map of an ecosystem. Include human structures (roads, ranches, parks, homes) separated by natural areas (forests, grassland, mountains). What are some potential strategies to limit habitat fragmentation in this area? Draw a protected area on the map and discuss your idea with the class.

Prevent Spread of Nonnative Species

In established ecosystems, community interactions between species lead to a dynamic balance of producers, composers, and decomposers. When a new species enters the ecosystem, it can upset this balance. The nonnative species may be able to use resources in the ecosystem better than native species do. By outcompeting native species, they can cause local extinctions of native species. For example, gardeners introduced kudzu vines to the American Southeast. They believed the vine was an excellent ground cover. Farmers also used the vine to reduce soil erosion. The creeping vine grows fast, especially in open areas. It thrives in humid, warm conditions. Once planted, it began to cover existing plants, depriving them of needed sunlight. Scientists now face the difficult task of controlling kudzu growth to protect plant diversity in affected ecosystems.

Kudzu competes with native plants for light and space. It can grow over large structures such as this bulldozer.

Reduce Pollution

Pollution of soil, air, and water harms many species and their habitats. Chemical pollutants are particularly dangerous because they are usually invisible. They can also travel great distances. Chemicals can build up in the communities they enter. They can build up in the bodies of plants and animals that absorb, ingest, or inhale them.

Some pollution sources include the burning of fossil fuels, fertilizers, pesticides, medicines, and litter. Noise and light produced by humans are also forms of pollution. They disrupt the normal actions of wildlife. For example, the noise from marine oil explorations affects the feeding and mating behaviors of whales.

Pollution can harm species directly and lead to habitat destruction. For example, it can cause contaminated drinking water, acid rain, algae blooms in lakes, and ocean garbage patches.

Under water, plastic bags look like jellyfish. Young sea turtles are at high risk of dying from eating these bags.

Reduce the Impact of Synthetic Materials

The life cycle of synthetic materials can affect biodiversity in different ways. *Synthetic materials* are human-made materials produced from natural materials. Plastic bags, fertilizer, and fuel are all examples of synthetic materials.

The life cycle of synthetic materials includes obtaining the materials from which a synthetic item will be made, and production, distribution, use, and disposal of the synthetic material. For example, plastic microbeads were once common in face washes and toothpastes. These microbeads are made from ethylene, a gas made from crude oil. Obtaining and transporting oil to make ethylene can lead to habitat destruction by land clearing and pollution from oil spills and processing, which can harm plants and animals and decrease biodiversity. Plastic microbeads that enter the environment through wastewater are not biodegradable and can be toxic to fish and wildlife. Plastic microbeads have been banned in some cosmetics.

plastic particles

A sample from the Great Pacific Garbage Patch, a gyre in the Pacific Ocean containing a high concentration of plastic particles and other debris. This plastic is sometimes mistaken for food by sea turtles and other marine animals.

17. Laysan albatrosses in the North Pacific Ocean eat squid and sunfish, but they sometimes mistake plastic for food. Albatross chicks that eat plastic may die. How might plastic pollution affect biodiversity in this area? Select all that apply.

   A. Populations of squid may increase.

   B. Populations of squid may decrease.

   C. Populations of species eaten by sunfish may decrease.

   D. Sunfish may become a predator of squid.

Case Study: Reducing the Impact of Synthetic Fertilizers

Nitrogen-based fertilizers provide plants with nitrogen, an essential nutrient. These fertilizers improve farm productivity, but their life cycle can have negative impacts on biodiversity and ecosystems.

Production This factory produces nitrogen-based fertilizer by converting nitrogen in the air into ammonia through a chemical reaction with hydrogen from natural gas. Greenhouse gases and dust emitted from fertilizer factories can pollute air, water, and soil.

Technologies to capture and reduce emissions can help reduce the impact of fertilizer production on local ecosystems.

Use Many farms rely on synthetic fertilizers to produce crops. Many people also use fertilizers in their lawns and gardens. But plants use only some of the nitrogen in fertilizer. Excess nitrogen is converted into nitrous oxide, a greenhouse gas that absorbs thermal energy in Earth's atmosphere and contributes to a rising global average temperature. Excess nitrogen can also enter groundwater, where it has the potential to contaminate drinking water and alter freshwater ecosystems.

Reducing the use of fertilizers or applying only the amount needed can help to reduce these effects on biodiversity and ecosystems.

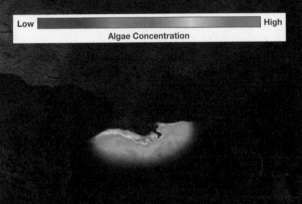

Low ▮▮▮▮▮▮▮▮▮▮▮▮ High
Algae Concentration

Disposal This satellite image shows the concentration of algae in the Gulf of Mexico. Fertilizer runoff from farms is carried in the Mississippi River to the Gulf, where it causes excess algal growth close to the shoreline. When the algae die, their decomposition depletes the water of oxygen, causing other marine animals to die or leave the area.

Planting cover crops such as clover to help recycle excess nutrients, using trees or shrubs on the edges of farms to filter runoff, and tilling fields less frequently can help to reduce the amount of fertilizer that enters streams and rivers.

18. Crop rotation is a method of farming in which crop types are alternated in order to preserve soil health and reduce the need for fertilizers and pesticides.

Increasing crop rotation on farms near the Mississippi River would likely lead to a(n) increase / decrease in fertilizer runoff and greater / less biodiversity where the river empties into the Gulf of Mexico.

19. Think of a synthetic material you use often. What are some impacts it could have on ecosystem services in your area or in other parts of the world? How can these impacts be reduced?

Put Strategies into Action

Reducing habitat loss and pollution requires solutions that involve individuals, businesses, cities, and nations. Scientific studies of these problems can describe their effects, but the studies alone cannot determine how to fix the problems. Societies must decide on those actions. For example, individuals can help reduce pollution in many ways. They can bike instead of drive and buy environmentally safe products. They can also recycle, reduce litter at home, or volunteer at environmental cleanups. Farmers can reduce pollution by finding ways to grow crops without pesticides. Businesses can conserve resources by using less paper, water, or fuel. Cities can reduce pollution by providing low-emission mass transportation. They can also set guidelines for acceptable light and noise levels. Finally, nations can help preserve ecosystem services through policies such as funding scientific research that addresses these issues and limiting overfishing and deforestation.

Case Study: Shark Bay Ecosystem

Decreases in shark populations affect many of the ecosystem services provided by ocean communities. Tiger sharks, sea cows, sea turtles, and seagrasses live in Western Australia's Shark Bay. The sharks prey on sea cows and turtles, which in turn eat seagrasses. Fish and shellfish depend on seagrasses for shelter from predators. In areas with few sharks, sea cows and sea turtles heavily graze seagrasses. This results in less habitat for shellfish, and fewer sites for fish to lay eggs and to grow while young. If sea cow and sea turtle populations were to grow too large, seagrass populations would collapse. As a result, shellfish and fish populations would decline and fisheries would lose profits. The loss of seagrasses also means fewer ocean plants to take up and store carbon. Excess carbon cycles back into the atmosphere and contributes to climate change.

Overfishing is the greatest threat to sharks, in Shark Bay and worldwide. Fisheries capture nearly 100 million sharks each year. Sharks can take more than 10 years to mature. Females give birth to only a few offspring, and do not give birth at all some years. So it takes a long time for shark populations to recover from overfishing. Australian conservation groups say protecting sharks is a priority. Their efforts include encouraging tourism to Shark Bay, which earns more profits than shark fishing. They are also setting catch limits and creating zones where shark fishing is not allowed.

Monitoring the healthy seagrass ecosystem in Shark Bay helps scientists identify ways to help threatened communities. This shark has been fitted with a camera and biosensor. They allow scientists to observe the shark's ecosystem interactions and monitor its behavior.

20. How does the health of shark populations affect the ecosystem services in the seagrass ecosystem? Select all that apply.

A. Sharks help carbon-capturing seagrasses thrive.

B. Sharks threaten sea cow and dolphin populations.

C. Sharks help protect fish populations for human use.

D. Sharks provide ecotourism opportunities.

21. What evidence in the text about Shark Bay suggests that a reduction in the tiger shark population has a large impact on the populations of other species?

EVIDENCE NOTEBOOK

22. Restoration efforts in the Everglades include developing marshes that filter pesticides flowing into the Everglades from farms farther north. How does this strategy directly affect wetland biodiversity and ecosystem services? Record your evidence.

Analyze the Spread of a Nonnative Species

Humans can accidentally transport species between distant ecosystems. For example, the emerald ash borer is a minor pest of trees in its native habitats in eastern Asia. However, it has destroyed millions of ash trees in the United States. It was first discovered in Michigan in 2002. It is native to Asia and likely came to the United States in wooden shipping crates. Ash tree destruction leaves gaps in forest canopies. Nonnative plants can grow in these brighter-light conditions. Damage to just one tree species may have long-lasting effects on many forest species.

Larvae of the emerald ash borer beetle feed on ash trees. They disrupt water and nutrient transport in the trees.

23. Nonnative species decrease / increase biodiversity by outcompeting native species for resources. They can also upset the balance of an ecosystem by decreasing / increasing the spread of diseases.

24. What are some ideas for technologies that conservationists might use to limit the spread of the emerald ash borer beetle? What might limit the implementation of these technologies?

_____

_____

_____

Evaluating Solutions for Maintaining Biodiversity

The most successful solutions to biodiversity loss meet the needs of ecosystems and of people. They protect biodiversity and ecosystem services while allowing people to meet their needs and maintain their quality of life. Some of these needs might conflict, but humans also benefit from healthy ecosystems. Understanding such needs and benefits encourages better collaboration among groups that develop and implement solutions.

Creative solutions help meet the needs of both humans and the environment. For example, fresh water is used to produce bottled water, juices, and other beverages. This use of fresh water reduces a limited natural resource. Beverage companies have partnered with conservation groups in watershed-protection efforts. The conservation groups work to restore and protect freshwater supplies using money donated by the beverage companies. Water quality and ecosystems within watersheds benefit from increased conservation efforts. The beverage companies benefit from tax breaks for their donations. They also create a more caring public image for consumers.

Monitor Biodiversity and Ecosystem Services

Effective solutions begin with understanding all parts of a problem. To understand threats to biodiversity, scientists must monitor changes to wildlife and ecosystem services. Some environmental factors are better indicators of the health of species and services than others, so this process begins with identifying factors to monitor.

Scientists then evaluate the best ways to gather data. They gather the data and analyze it carefully to identify the causes of decreases in biodiversity and ecosystem services in an area. Scientists conduct research to compare past and present data collected from ecosystems. They look for changes in ecosystem populations, resources, and services.

This scientist gathers data about water quality. The information will be analyzed to determine if conservation efforts are needed.

25. When human activities threaten ecosystem services, why is monitoring needed to design successful solutions? Select all that apply.

   A. to determine the severity of the problem

   B. to provide data for fundraising efforts

   C. to correctly identify causes of declines in ecosystem services

   D. to prioritize criteria for conservation efforts

Define Criteria of the Design Problem

Maintaining biodiversity and ecosystem services can be challenging, particularly when the needs of ecosystems conflict with those of humans. Ideally, solutions to such conflicts will address human needs and ecosystem needs. For example, in California, nearly 90 percent of floodplain, river, and seasonal wetland habitats have been lost to farming and city growth. Scientists agree that urban forests can help restore some of the services, such as stormwater runoff control and water filtration, provided by these habitats. Urban forests also provide shade and visual beauty. But urban areas need open space for roads, parking lots, and playing fields, and they may have dry climates that cannot support trees that need lots of watering. Such needs and limitations must be clearly defined and carefully considered.

Volunteers plant trees on a residential street to help increase the number of urban trees in Richmond, California.

There are many ways to increase urban tree plantings, but only some of these solutions will successfully address the problem. The *criteria* are the features a potential solution must have in order to work. Defining criteria as precisely as possible helps to ensure a successful solution. In this case, the criteria may include that the trees should be native species that require little watering. Other criteria might be that the trees should not change how parks are used, or that falling leaves must not create safety hazards for pedestrians and drivers. Some of these criteria focus on meeting the needs of the ecosystem. Others aim to meet the needs of people. Identifying the solutions that best meet the criteria is the next step in solving the design problem.

Define Constraints of the Design Problem

Designing effective solutions also requires considering environmental, economic, scientific, and social factors that affect the solution. These factors help to identify any limits the solution must work within. They are called *constraints*. Solutions that do not meet all the constraints of the design problem cannot be used. For example, an exciting design solution cannot be used if it is too expensive. One constraint of the urban forest problem could be that the canopy of mature trees must be less than 9 meters (about 30 feet) wide to protect road visibility and keep paths safe. Another limit is that established tree species must be able to survive periods with little water since watering restrictions will limit the amount of extra water the trees can get during dry weather.

26. What are some examples of social factors that city planners would need to consider before agreeing on a tree planting program in an urban area?

EVIDENCE NOTEBOOK

27. Restoring wetlands involves reclaiming existing ranches and farmland. What are the costs and benefits of this solution for humans and ecosystem services? Record your evidence.

Case Study: Mountain Meadow Restoration

When trying to maintain biodiversity and ecosystem services, decision makers evaluate how well each proposed solution meets the criteria and constraints of the design problem. This step helps them decide which solution will be the most successful.

Recently, the water levels in California's reservoirs were at historically low levels, due to a long drought. Restoring the degraded mountain meadow ecosystems in California's Sierra Nevada watersheds is one proposed solution to help retain water. Meadow plants slow the flow of rainwater and melted snow. Water can then soak into the ground. This prevents flooding and erosion. It also improves the reliability and quality of water flow to streams and reservoirs. It is a long-term drought solution.

However, there are serious barriers to the success of mountain meadow restoration programs. Ranchers living in mountain areas do not support the programs because they reduce available grazing land. Restoration requires many workers, takes many years, and needs long-term monitoring. Also, measuring the positive benefits of meadow restoration is difficult. This makes funding hard to obtain. Government leaders prefer solutions to the water shortage problem that provide immediate, measurable results.

Conservation engineers added a trail above this mountain meadow in Yosemite National Park. The trail helps protect the meadow's plant life from people.

28. Mountain meadow restoration is a chosen solution to water shortages in California. Consider each of the criteria listed in the table. Rank the criteria on a scale from 1 to 4, with 4 being the most important. Then explain your reasoning.

Criteria for Mountain Meadow Restoration Projects in the Sierra Nevada	
Criteria	Ranking
Increase native species diversity in the restored area	
Encourage growth of plants that attract birds and pollinators	
Involve volunteer organizations to lower costs and provide workers	
Include regular sampling to determine progress and success	
Explain your reasoning:	

Evaluate Proposed Design Solutions

Once restored, a new mountain meadow could fail. For example, pine trees around the meadow could spread into the area. Pine trees crowd out meadow plants. They increase shade that discourages new growth. There are several solutions to the spread of pine trees into meadows.

One option is to use prescribed burns to remove the trees. Intense fires damage ecosystems by destroying plants and changing soil chemistry, but small fires do little damage, especially if the plants in the fire area are wet.

A second option is to bulldoze pine trees that sprout and remove new saplings each winter. Removing trees on top of snow minimizes the disturbance of soil. This prevents loose soil from being washed away by water. If the soil washes into reservoirs, it would take up the water space and reduce water quality.

There are other possible options to control pine tree growth. Fences could be installed. Native, dense shrubs could be planted to make a physical barrier, so that animals could not carry fertilized cones into the meadow.

29. Use the decision matrix to score the proposed solutions to remove pine trees from the meadow. Use the criteria rankings you did earlier to help you score. For example, if you gave a "4" to "increase native species diversity in the restored area," then score each proposed solution on a scale of 0–4. Base the score on how well the solution meets that criterion. For the criterion that scored a "3," proposed solutions will be scored from 0–3. Use this same process for the criteria ranked "2" and "1." When done, total the score for each solution. Identify the most successful one.

Decision Matrix: Solutions to Reduce the Spread of Pine Trees into Restored Mountain Meadows

Proposed solutions	Increase native species	Encourage birds and pollinators	Involve volunteer organizations	Include regular sampling	Total score
1. Use prescribed burns					
2. Winter-time tree removal					
3. Use barbed-wire fencing					
4. Use native-shrub barrier					

30. Think about your top-scoring solution. What are likely cost and social constraints that might need to be met when putting the solution into action?

adeoffs

...ution priorities conflict with one
...his case, tradeoffs must be accepted
...t a solution. For example, a criterion for
...g mountain meadows is to keep cost as low
...ssible. To meet this criterion, a lot of volunteer
...p is needed. Volunteers likely lack the experience
of experts, so the project will likely run longer than
expected. Therefore, accepting that the project will
take longer to complete is a fair tradeoff to reduce
costs as much as possible. Another tradeoff might
include accepting the increased difficulty and cost
of controlling pines in the snow rather than in spring
or summer.

    Some solutions might no longer work as
conditions change. Sometimes, unexpected issues
cause the problem to be redefined. Suppose several
native shrubs that are moved to the meadow carry
a disease, which spreads rapidly. This creates a new
problem that needs to be solved to preserve the
meadow. New criteria and constraints need to be
identified. Then new solutions can be considered.

Off-road enthusiasts discover a mountain meadow.
Restoration plans had to shift to address the new threat
to the meadow's health.

Identify a Solution

Decision makers looking for a solution to biodiversity loss often choose solutions that
optimize the balance between benefits and cost. The best solution is often the one that
addresses biodiversity loss directly by enacting laws. For example, overfishing is the
primary threat to tiger sharks. A solution to the decline of shark populations that involves
an immediate reduction in shark fishing would likely be prioritized over solutions that
involve protecting sharks' breeding areas only.

31. Conservation groups and governments have limited budgets to fund projects.
Which of the following solutions is most likely to be chosen to preserve biodiversity?

    A. the one with the fewest constraints

    B. the one that provides the most benefits at the lowest cost

    C. the one that best meets criteria and constraints, regardless of cost

    D. the one that most improves biodiversity

32. Suppose ranchers near a mountain meadow lobby local officials for grazing rights.
Their lobbying disrupts plans for meadow conservation. How does this show that
science contributes to understanding biodiversity loss and its possible solutions,
but it does not dictate decisions that society makes?

_____

_____

_____

_____

Continue Your Exploration

Name: _____   Date: _____

Check out the path below or go online to choose one of the other paths shown.

| Careers in Science | • **Backyard Biodiversity**
• **Hands-On Labs** 🖐
• **Propose Your Own Path** | *Go online to choose one of these other paths.* |

Ecotourism

The ecotourism industry tries to provide exciting natural experiences for travelers. Their goal is to preserve habitats and increase awareness of threats to biodiversity. However, it is a challenge to provide tours to wildlife areas without disrupting protection efforts. Ecotourism companies can maximize benefits to ecosystems by working with governments, conservation groups, scientists, and citizens to design their programs.

Case Study: Elephant Conservation in Thailand

Elephants have played an essential role in the industry and culture of Thailand for centuries. Most of these elephants were captured to work in the logging industry. Then, logging was banned. Elephant caretakers (called *mahouts*) began working with their elephants in the entertainment and tourism industries. Not all elephants and mahouts do well in this new work, as care for the elephants is inconsistent and pay for mahouts can be low.

The elephant population in Thailand now includes about 5,000 animals. Only 20% live in the wild. Many elephants live in camps run by conservation groups or by people hoping to earn money by providing interactions with elephants. The camps are popular ecotourism destinations. Yet, some of them focus on tourism more than conservation. Many fail to meet the needs of elephants or mahouts. Ecotourism to those locations may encourage elephant interactions with people that conservationists want to prevent.

Ecotourism activities, such as elephant viewing, can help conservation efforts when their impact on wildlife is minimized.

Continue Your Exploration

The Elephant Nature Park (ENP) in northern Thailand is an example of how ecotourism can help biodiversity. ENP's mission criteria include being a sanctuary for endangered species, providing rainforest restoration, preserving native culture, and providing visitor education. The park is opposed to elephant shows or rides. It is home to more than 35 elephants and has cared for 200 more, returning them to the wild. ENP is supported financially by visitors, who pay to work at the camp and to care for the elephants.

1. ENP collaborates with conservation groups, Thailand's government, and local monks. The government provides funding and lands. The monks bless trees planted by the park, which discourages illegal logging. What does this tell you about how human culture and conservation efforts influence each other?

2. Inspired by ENP, other elephant camps are changing their ways. They are getting rid of elephant shows to focus on care and conservation. How is this evidence that ENP is meeting its mission criteria?

3. When evaluating the conservation success of the Elephant Nature Park, what additional information would you like to have? Can you rely on the information provided here about elephant conservation in Thailand? Why or why not?

4. **Collaborate** Imagine there is a natural resource in your community that needs protection from heavy tourist traffic. Brainstorm ecotourism-based solutions to this problem. With your group, develop criteria and choose one solution that meets the needs of people and the ecosystem. Present your solution to the class as a brief oral report.

Can You Explain It?

Name: _____   Date: _____

How can we develop a solution to biodiversity loss in the Everglades without shutting humans out of this endangered ecosystem?

EVIDENCE NOTEBOOK

Refer to the notes in your Evidence Notebook to help you construct an explanation for how to develop a strategy for maintaining biodiversity in the Everglades without shutting humans out.

1. State your claim. Make sure your claim fully explains what decision makers should consider and the steps engineers should take in designing a solution.

2. Summarize the evidence you have gathered to support your claim and explain your reasoning.

Checkpoints

Answer the following questions to check your understanding of the lesson.

Use the photo of a banana plantation to answer Question 3.

3. Banana plantations are planted in tropical forests. They displace other native plants. Bananas are harvested from the same plants year after year. What do banana plantations do in the ecosystem? Select all that apply.

   A. decrease biodiversity in the area

   B. increase natural resources

   C. reduce water pollution

   D. impact ecosystem services

4. Undisturbed polar ecosystems naturally have less biodiversity than undisturbed tropical rainforest ecosystems. Which of the following statements are true?

   A. Polar ecosystems are less healthy than tropical rainforest ecosystems.

   B. Polar ecosystems are home to fewer species than tropical rain forests.

   C. As long as they remain undisturbed, both ecosystems are equally "healthy."

   D. Polar ecosystems are less important than tropical rain forests.

5. Scientific understanding of biodiversity issues caused by overfishing can / cannot describe the consequences of continued overfishing. However, such knowledge does / does not identify the decisions society should make.

Use the photo of a protected habitat to answer Question 6.

6. Suppose people ignore a sign like this one. What might happen if they walk into the protected area? Select all that apply.

   A. increased water pollution due to littering

   B. destruction of turtle habitats

   C. increased participation in conservation efforts

   D. spread of a nonnative species

7. A wetland provides flood control services. Engineers are evaluating competing design solutions to preserve this service. What should they consider?

   A. the number of predators in the ecosystem

   B. the amount of impermeable ground cover (ground cover that does not soak up precipitation) in the ecosystem

   C. the best native plants to plant in the project area

   D. the number of pollinators in the project area

Interactive Review

Complete this page to review the main concepts of the lesson.

Humans depend on healthy ecosystems. Biodiversity is directly related to ecosystem health.

A. Explain why humans depend on healthy ecosystems for resources and services.

Strategies to maintain biodiversity include protecting habitats and individual species, reducing the impact of synthetic materials, and preventing the spread of nonnative species.

B. Explain how protecting habitats helps to maintain biodiversity.

Monitoring ecosystems allows scientists to develop solutions that help maintain biodiversity and ecosystem services. Choosing the best solution involves evaluating how well a possible solution meets the criteria and constraints of the problem.

C. When should scientists collect data about ecosystem biodiversity and services?

Choose one of the activities to explore how this unit connects to other topics.

People in Science

John Paul Balmonte, Aquatic Microbial Ecologist

Born in the Philippines and raised in California, John Paul Balmonte is a member of the LGBTQ+ community and was the first person in his family to get a PhD. His studies of bacteria in aquatic ecosystems have taken him all over the world. Bacteria play many crucial roles in ecosystems as both producers and decomposers. Balmonte uses DNA sequencing to learn more about the types and functions of bacteria in lakes, rivers, and oceans.

Research a type of microorganism that is important to an aquatic ecosystem. What is its role in the ecosystem? Present your findings to the class.

Engineer It

Permeable Pavers Stormwater runoff can lead to flooding and increased water pollution. Water that flows over roads, parking lots, and driveways can carry pollutants into bodies of water instead of being absorbed into soils. Permeable pavers were designed to reduce the amount of stormwater runoff.

Identify an area that has an issue with stormwater runoff. Research permeable pavers and at least two other design solutions for reducing runoff. Evaluate each solution based on the needs of your chosen area. Based on your analysis, recommend a solution and present your findings.

Technology Connection

Camera Traps in Wildlife Research A camera trap takes a photo when an animal triggers its infrared sensor. Camera traps have provided important data related to wildlife conservation. Examples include evidence that Javan rhinos are breeding, a record of the first wolverine in California since 1922, and evidence that Siamese crocodiles still inhabit Cambodia. Data related to the range and size of populations are important for designing solutions to maintain biodiversity.

Research the benefits and limitations of camera traps. Investigate a case in which camera traps are being used to study a species or ecosystem. Create a pamphlet that explains how these data can help to maintain biodiversity.

A cougar caught on film by a camera trap in Wyoming.

Name: **Date:**

Complete this review to check your understanding of the unit.

Use the map to answer Questions 1 and 2.

1. Which part of the United States has the highest biodiversity of reptiles?

    A. Northwest

    B. Northeast

    C. South

    D. Midwest

2. Purple / Red / Orange regions on the map would likely be most affected by the removal of one reptile species. In general, areas with higher / lower biodiversity remain more stable, recovering more / less quickly after a disturbance.

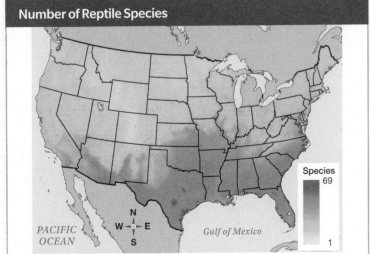

Number of Reptile Species

Species
69

1

Credit: Adapted from "US protected lands mismatch biodiversity priorities" by Clinton N. Jenkins, et al, from *PNAS*, v. 112, no. 16, April 21, 2015. Reprinted by permission of PNAS.

3. Paclitaxel is a powerful anticancer drug that can be made from a chemical compound found in European yew trees. Paclitaxel is an example of a natural / synthetic material. Overharvesting populations of European yew trees without replenishing them would likely have a positive / negative impact on society.

Use this graph of coastal dead zones to answer Questions 4 and 5.

4. The amount of coastal dead zones increased / decreased between 1980 and 2010.

5. Biodiversity in these coastal dead zones is high / low. Therefore, the ecosystem health of these areas would be considered high / low.

Coastal Dead Zones Worldwide

Dead zones are areas in the ocean where the oxygen level in the deep water is so low that most organisms cannot live there. Fertilizer runoff is a major cause of dead zones in the ocean.

Source: Convention on Biological Diversity, *Global Biodiversity Outlook 3* (2010): 60.

6. Complete the table by adding information about the features, stability, and impact of ecosystems with high and low biodiversity.

Ecosystem Biodiversity	Features	Stability	Impacts on Society
High Biodiversity	An ecosystem with high biodiversity has a high variety of species, in terms of the number of species and genetic variation within each species. Ecosystems with high biodiversity can generally recover relatively quickly from a disturbance.		
Low Biodiversity			

Name: _____   Date: _____

Use the image of the farm to answer Questions 7–10.

Farm Ecosystem

 Plant diversity A variety of plant species increases the health of soil by providing different nutrients.

 Earthworms Decomposers return nutrients from nonliving plant and animal matter back to the soil.

 Bacteria Some bacteria change nitrogen gas into forms of nitrogen that plants can use.

 Fungi Mycorrhizal fungi help provide plant roots with water and mineral nutrients.

7. Describe the ecosystem services provided by the diverse soil community shown in this farm ecosystem.

8. What might be the impacts on this farm if soil biodiversity decreased?

9. The forested area behind this farm became fragmented when the land was cleared for farming. How might this habitat fragmentation affect biodiversity in the forest?

10. In what ways could biodiversity be maintained on the farm and the surrounding ecosystems?

Use the image of the mangroves to answer Questions 11–13.

Mangrove Trees

Mangroves naturally filter runoff.

Mangroves dissipate wave energy during storms, which reduces flooding.

Mangroves provide shelter and breeding grounds for many organisms.

Mangrove roots are well-anchored, preventing erosion.

11. What are some ways that mangrove trees promote biodiversity?

12. What are some ecosystem services that mangroves provide to humans?

13. How would this ecosystem be affected if many of the mangrove trees were removed?

Name: Date:

What is the best way to prevent shoreline erosion?

Humans have developed many solutions to try to prevent shoreline erosion. Compare the shorelines of these two images. In the image on the left, natural vegetation has been maintained along the lake shoreline. In the image on the right, the natural vegetation has been replaced with a stone wall. Research the strengths and weaknesses of each of these solutions, including how each solution might impact biodiversity and ecosystem services. Then make a recommendation to a homeowner on a similar lake who is considering both options. Write a report that highlights your findings.

The steps below will help guide your research and develop your recommendation.

Engineer It

1. **Define the Problem** Why is it important to prevent shoreline erosion along a lake? Define criteria and constraints of a design solution for preventing shoreline erosion. As you define the problem, consider that the lake is used for swimming, boating, fishing, and watching wildlife.

Engineer It

2. **Conduct Research** Compare and contrast the use of natural vegetation and a stone wall for preventing erosion along a shoreline. What are the strengths and weaknesses of each solution?

3. **Construct an Explanation** Explain how each solution would affect the biodiversity and ecosystem services for the lake ecosystem. How might a small change to one component of an ecosystem produce a large change in another component of the ecosystem?

4. **Recommend a Solution** Evaluate each solution based on how well they meet the criteria and constraints. Based on your evaluation, recommend one of these solutions for a homeowner who is considering both options.

5. **Communicate** Write a report that explains your evidence and reasoning for the recommended solution.

✓ **Self-Check**

	I defined the problem, including identifying criteria and constraints for the design solution.
	I conducted research to learn about two solutions for preventing shoreline erosion — natural vegetation and stone walls.
	I constructed an explanation for how each solution would affect biodiversity and ecosystem services in a lake ecosystem.
	I recommended a solution for a homeowner considering both options.
	I communicated the evidence and reasoning for my recommendation in a report.

Go online to access the **Interactive Glossary**. *You can use this online tool to look up definitions for all the vocabulary terms in this book.*

Pronunciation Key

Sound	Symbol	Example	Respelling	Sound	Symbol	Example	Respelling
ă	a	pat	PAT	ŏ	ah	bottle	BAHT'l
ā	ay	pay	PAY	ō	oh	toe	TOH
âr	air	care	KAIR	ô	aw	caught	KAWT
ä	ah	father	FAH•ther	ôr	ohr	roar	ROHR
är	ar	argue	AR•gyoo	oi	oy	noisy	NOYZ•ee
ch	ch	chase	CHAYS	ōō	u	book	BUK
ĕ	e	pet	PET	ōō	oo	boot	BOOT
ĕ (at end of a syllable)	eh	settee lessee	seh•TEE leh•SEE	ou	ow	pound	POWND
ĕr	ehr	merry	MEHR•ee	s	s	center	SEN•ter
ē	ee	beach	BEECH	sh	sh	cache	CASH
g	g	gas	GAS	ŭ	uh	flood	FLUHD
ĭ	i	pit	PIT	ûr	er	bird	BERD
ĭ (at end of a syllable)	ih	guitar	gih•TAR	z	z	xylophone	ZY•luh•fohn
ī	y eye (only for a complete syllable)	pie island	PY EYE•luhnd	z	z	bags	BAGZ
îr	ir	hear	HIR	zh	zh	decision	dih•SIZH •uhn
j	j	germ	JERM	ə	uh	around broken focus	uh•ROWND BROH•kuhn FOH•kuhs
k	k	kick	KIK	ər	er	winner	WIN•er
ng	ng	thing	THING	th	th	thin they	THIN THAY
ngk	ngk	bank	BANGK	w	w	one	WUHN
				wh	hw	whether	HWETH•er

R1

Index

Page numbers for key terms are in **boldface** type.
Page numbers in *italic* type indicate illustrative material, such as photographs, graphs, charts, and maps.

A

abiotic resource
  abundant, 374, 375
  limited, 372, *372*
abrasion, in weathering process,
  269, *269*, 272, 273
abundant resources
  abiotic, 374, 375
  biotic, 374, 375
  predicting effects of, 374–376
acetic acid, *113*, 114—115, 163
acid rain, 204, 218, *218*, 270
Act, 78, 167, 207, 349, 391
active volcano, 452, 474
  Kilauea, 455–456, *455, 456*, 473,
    473
  Mauna Loa, Hawaii, 474–475, *475*
Adélie penguin, 523
aggregate, 10, *10*, 13, *13*, 36, *36*
agricultural practices, soil impacts,
  349, *349*
agriculture, ecosystem
  disturbances caused by, 532
Aialik Bay, Alaska, 544, *544*
air, as matter, 54
airbag, 149–150, *149, 150*
airbag helmet, 28, *28*
air pressure, elevation changing,
  97, 103
Alaska, tectonic plates in, 333, *333*
algae
  as biofuel, 257, *257*
  for biomass fuel production, 211,
    211, 213, *213*
  as biotic factor, 372
  feeding relationships, 384, 385–
    387, *385*
  photosynthesis in, 256
  phototrophs, 243
  producer transform sun energy into
    food, 236, *236*

algal bloom, 374, *374*
  effects of, 550
  in Gulf of Mexico, 575
alligator, 364, *364*, 365
Alligator Rivers region, Australia,
  368, *368*
alluvial fan, 282, *282*, 432, *432*
aluminum
  life cycle of, 9, *9*
Amazon rain forest, 565
amino acids, 251
ammonia, 154, *154*
ammonium chloride, 183, *183*,
  185–186
amoeba, 366, *366*
amorphous silicon, 120, *120*
amphibolite, 297, *297*
analogy, 234
analysis
  of bicycle helmet designs, 30–31,
    30–31
  of biodiversity, 530–531
  of change of state, 88
  of chemical equations, 159–164
  of continental data, 320–323
  ecosystem energy flow, 402–406
  of habitat fragmentation, 572
  of impact of synthetic material,
    500–505, *500–505*
  of interactions within Earth system,
    428–431
  of molecules, 115
  natural hazard, historical data on,
    450–451, *450*
  of natural resources used to create
    synthetic materials,
    196–199
  of natural systems and chemical
    reactions, 138–139
  of ocean-floor data,
    324–327
  of states of matter, 73–74

of substances before and after
    chemical reaction changes,
    146–148
  of synthetic material design,
    210–212
  of thermal energy used in chemical
    processes, 179–183
anemone, clownfish and, 389, *389*
anglerfish, 391, *391*
animal
  as biotic factor, 372
  competition among, 393, *393*
  consumers of, 237
  decomposition of dead, 237
  feeding relationship of, 385–387,
    385, 388, 394
  impact of resource use on, 15
  plastics impact on, 516, *516*
  sunlight as energy source for, 233–
    234, 256–257, *256*
anole lizard, 393, *393*
Antarctica, 523
anteater, 237, *237*
apple, 235, *235*
aquifer
  contamination, synthetic material
    production, 502, *502*
  groundwater, 347, *347*, 352
  model recharge and withdrawal
    from, 353–354, *353*
Aral Sea, shrinking, 352, *352*
Arches National Park, 284, *284*
Arctic, oil drilling in, 416, *416*
arctic ecosystem
  biodiversity in, 564
  disappearing sea ice in, 50, *50*
argument
  constructing, 537
  from evidence, 36, 255, 304, 375,
    387, 440, 569
  supporting, 231

Arizona

Barringer Meteorite Crater, 427, *427*, 487, *487*

meteorite crater, 427, *427*, 441, *441*

South Coyote Buttes Wilderness area, 268, *268*

Army Corps of Engineers, 37–38, *37–38*

Art Connection

Working with Wax, 126

ash tree, 577, *577*

Asian carp, 394, *394*

aspirin, 209, *209*

Assessment

Lesson Self-Check, 19–21, 39–41, 67–69, 81–83, 101–103, 123–125, 151–153, 171–173, 191–193, 215–217, 245–247, 263–265, 281–283, 305–307, 337–339, 357–359, 379–381, 397–398, 413–415, 441–443, 463–465, 489–491, 513–515, 541–543, 559–561, 585–587

Unit Performance Task, 47–48, 131–132, 223–224, 313–314, 421–422, 521–522, 593–594

Unit Review, 43–46, 127–130, 219–222, 309–312, 417–420, 517–520, 589–592

asteroid

Barringer Meteorite Crater, Arizona, 427, *427*, 487, *487*

biggest known Earth impacts, 488, *488*

impact prediction, 487–488, *487–488*

potentially hazardous asteroid (PHA), 487–488, *487–488*

Atlantic cod population, 536, *536*

atmosphere in Earth system, 429, *429*

atom

balanced chemical equation, checking, 166

bond to form molecule, 232, *232*

as building blocks of matter, 231–232

carbon as building block of living things, 251–252

in chemical formula, 156

in complex molecules, 115–117

compounds of, 109–110, *109*, *110*, 125, *125*

of elements, 108, *108*

law of conservation of matter, 165

mineral formation, 286

in molecules, 112

organisms and nonliving things made of, 104–120

particles of matter, 107, *107*

in simple molecules, 113

structure affected by connections of, 119

avalanche, prediction, 468, *468*

avocado, lipids in, 252, *252*

B

bacteria

as biotic factor, 372

exponential growth pattern, 377, *377*

nitrogen-fixing, 389

photosynthesis in, 256

phototrophs, 243

producer transform sun energy into food, 236, *236*

baking soda and vinegar chemical reaction, 144, *144*, 163

balanced chemical equation, 165, 166–168, 169–170

bamboo, renewable source, 202, *202*

bananas, 537, 586, *586*

Banff National Park, Canada, 426, *426*

Bangladesh, *553*

Barbary macaque, 528, *528*

Barringer, Daniel Moreau, 427, *427*

Barringer Meteorite Crater, Arizona, 427, *427*, 487, *487*

basalt

as igneous rock, 290, *290*

metamorphic rock formation, 297, *297*

bat, 59, *59*

beach erosion, 272, *272*

bear, *56*

beaver, 401, *401*, 413, *413*

bee

biodiversity of, 530, *530*

cross-pollination by, 390, *390*

importance of, 549

Bezeau, Robert, 23, *23*

bicycle

balanced equation for, 169

helmet design, 26, *26*, 27, *27*, 29, 30–31, 41, *41*

materials used to make, 206, *206*

biodiesel fuel, 213

biodiversity, 529

of bird species, 534, *534*

causes of loss of, 568–569

description of, 528–531, 543

ecosystem dynamics and, 523–594

ecosystem health indicated by, 526–538, 587

in ecosystem recovery, 533

evaluating loss of, 564–569

in Everglades, 563, *563*

human creativity preserving, 562, *562*

human influences on, 535–538

loss of affecting ecosystem health, 567–569

maintaining, 562–582

measuring, 530–531

monitoring and preserving, 538, 578, 587

negative impact on, 536–537

patterns in, 531

protecting, 537

solutions for maintaining, 578–582

strategies for maintaining, 570–577

types of, 529

biofuel, 213–214, *213*, *214*

algae as, 257, *257*

biomass, 201, 213, 347, *347*

biomass engineer, 213–214, *213*

biomimicry, 42, *42*

bioremediation, 240, *240*

biosensor, *576*

biosphere

Earth system, 6, 429, *429*

tabletop, 225

biotic resources
abundant, 374, 375
limited, 372–373
bird
biodiversity of, 534, *534*
oil spill impact on, 205, *205*, 501, *501*
bison, 536
bleaching, 570, *570*
blizzard, 449, *449*
boiling point, 89, *89*, *98*, 141
Bosch, Carl, 189–190, *189*, *190*
brainstorming, 25, *25*, 28, *28*
breccia, 292, *292*
bromine, 71, *71*, 81, *81*
Brown, Robert, 62
Brownian motion, 62
buckthorn, 536
bumblebee, 530, *530*
Burmese python, 536, *536*
burros, 532, *532*

C

calcite
hardness of, 57
in marble formation, 299, *299*
as sedimentary cement, 292, *292*
calcium, 231, *231*
calcium carbonate
limestone, 294, *294*, 295, *295*
sedimentary rock formation, 59, *59*, 294, *294*
caldera, 439, *439*, 440, *440*
California
Clear Lake wildfire, 444, *444*
Griffith Park in Los Angeles, 524, *524*
mountain meadow restoration, 580–581
Oak Woodland Regeneration, 557–558, *558*
San Francisco Bay, 126
Sierra Nevada, 580
Silicon Valley, 126
Sonoran Desert, 532, *532*
urbanization of, 579
water levels in, 580
Yosemite National Park, 291

canyon
formation, 278, *278*, 285, *285*, 294, *294*, 305, *305*
underwater, 318, *318*
Can You Explain It? 5, 19, 23, 39, 53, 67, 71, 81, 85, 101, 105, 123, 137, 151, 155, 171, 175, 191, 195, 215, 229, 245, 249, 263, 267, 281, 285, 305, 319, 337, 341, 357, 361, 379, 383, 397, 401, 413, 427, 441, 445, 463, 467, 489, 493, 513, 527, 541, 545, 559, 563, 585
carbon
as building block of living things, 251–252
carbon-based molecules in cells, 251–252, *252*
carbon cycle, 408, *408*
in complex molecules, 115, *115*
in diamonds, 106, 116, *116*, 119, *119*
in graphite, 119, *119*
in humans, 105, *105*, 231, *231*, 232
in propane, 105, *105*
carbon cycle, 408, *408*
carbon dioxide
alcoholic fermentation, 261
in cellular respiration, 258–259, *258*
chemosynthesis, 243
lactic acid fermentation, 261, *261*
molecule of, 232, *232*
photosynthesis producing, 236, *236*, 256, *256*
plants using, 532, *532*
removal of as ecosystem service, 7, *7*
and water to form carbonic acid, 251, *251*
from wood burning, 58
carbon fiber life cycle, 510
carbonic acid, 251, *251*
carbon monoxide, 113
carbon removal tower, 409, *409*
Careers in Engineering: Biomass Engineer, 213–214, *213*
Careers in Engineering: Civil Engineer, 37–38
Careers in Engineering: Materials Engineer, 511–512, *511*

Careers in Science: Ecotourism, 583–584
Careers in Science: Forensics, 99–100
Careers in Science: Restoration Ecologist, 539–540
carnivore, feeding relationships, 384, 385–387, *385*
Case Study
Bicycle Helmet, 27, *27*
Elephant Conservation in Thailand, 583–584
Mountain Meadow Restoration, 580–581
Reducing the Impact of Synthetic Fertilizers, 575
Shark Bay Ecosystem, 576–577
cassiterite, 201, *201*
catalyst, in chemical reaction, 182, *182*
categories of matter, 55
cause and effect
chain, 569
constructing statements of, 527
diagram, *376*
relationship, 43, 359
statement, 527
table of, *44*, *393*
cave, ecosystem of, 59, *59*
cavefish, 59, *59*
Cave of Crystals, Mexico, 52, *52*
cell phone
case for, 24
design, 24, 26
natural resources for, 6, *6*
recycling, 504, *504*
synthetic material life cycle example, 496–497, *496–497*, 500, *500*, 502, 506, *506*
cells
carbon-based molecules in, 251–252, *252*
energy production for, 248–265
photosynthesis for energy production, 253–258

© Houghton Mifflin Harcourt Publishing Company

crop
 biodiversity lacking in, 537
 consumer use, 12, *12*
 demand on, 12, *12*
 from farming, 9, *9*
 production and distribution of, 10, *10*
 reintroducing wild genes in, 537
 resource availability, 200, *200*
 rotation of, 349, *349*, 575
cross-pollination by bees, 390, *390*
crude oil, 15, *15*
crystal, *286*
 mineral formation, 286, 287
 model formation of, lab, 289
 time scale, igneous rock formation, 290, *290*
crystalline silicon, 120, *120*
crystals, 116, *116*
Cusatis, Ginluca, 65–66, *65*
Cynognathus, 320, *320*
cytoplasm, cellular respiration in, 258
Czech Republic, 527, *527*

D

Dalton, John, 61
dam, hydroelectric, 347
data
 analyzing and interpreting, 35
 continental data, 320–323
 fossil data, 320–321, *320*, *321*, 323
 landform data, 322, *322*, 342, *342*, 343, *343*
 from monitoring natural hazards, 469, *469*, 471, 474–475, 480
 natural hazard, 450–451, *450*
 ocean-floor data analysis, 324–327
 tornado, interpreting patterns in, 458–460
 volcanic, interpreting patterns in, 452–457
dead zone, 589, *589*
decision matrix, 581
decomposer, 237, *237*, 533

decomposition
 bioremediation, 240, *240*
 as biotic factor, 372
 carbon cycle, 408, *408*
 cycle of energy and matter, 229, 237–240, *237*, *238*, *239*
 ecosystem services of, 566, *566*
 by fungus, 236, *236*
 nitrogen cycle, 409, *409*
deep-ocean trenches, 324, *324*, 325, 327
Deepwater Horizon offshore drilling rig, 501, *501*
deer, population change in, 375, *375*
deforestation, 349, *349*, 557
 for coffee plantations, 567, *567*
delta, river, 273, *273*, 435, *435*, 517, *517*
density
 measure of mass and volume, 64
 as physical property of matter, 141
density of matter, 57
deoxyribonucleic acid (DNA), 117
deposition, 272
 agents of, 272–275
 energy driving process of, 272–278
 gravity as agent of, 274, *274*
 ice as agent of, 274, *274*
 rock cycle model, 301–302, *301*
 time scale, 278, *278*
 water as agent of, 272–275, *273–275*
 wind as agent of, 272–274, *273*
desert
 ecosystem of, 364, 528
 sand in, 36, *36*
 water supply in, 56
desert locust, 545, 559, *559*
design, of synthetic materials, 210–212
design problem. *See also* **engineering problem**
 defining constraints, 579
 defining criteria of, 579
 in real-life, 32, *32*
design process
 evaluate design solutions, 581
 identifying solutions, 2, *2*, 24, 36, 522, 582
 solution tradeoffs, 582

desire
 identifying, 26, *26*
 met by synthetic materials, 495
Devils Tower, Wyoming, 291, *291*
diagram
 of airbag design, *150*
 of carbon-based molecules, *265*
 of carbon cycle, *408*
 cause and effect, *376*
 of cellular respiration and photosynthesis, *260*
 of chemical formulas of minerals, *158*, *166*
 of chemical reaction rate variables, *182*
 of cycling of matter, *410*
 of diamond structure, *116*
 of earthquake warning system, *336*
 of elements and compounds, *111*
 of engineering design process, 25, *25*
 of fish and crab relationships, *376*
 of food chain, *403*
 of formation of polyethylene, *207*
 of landfill exposure pathways, *520*
 of molecular models, *112*, *113*
 of ocean floor, *324*, *327*
 of pencil production, *45*
 of plate boundaries and surface features, *329*
 of plate movement, *334*
 of rock cycle, *301*, *307*
 of soil formation, *344*
 Venn diagram, *551*
 of volcanic hazards, *454*
 of water molecule, *124*, *157*
 of weathering and erosion, *342*
 of web design process, *46*
 of Yellowstone Caldera area, *440*
diamond, 116, *116*, 119, *119*
 chemical formula for, 158, *158*
 synthetic, 500, *500*
digestion, chemistry of, 218
dinosaur, 230, *230*
 matching fossil data across Atlantic, 320–321, *320*, *321*
Dirzo, Rodolfo, 557–558, *557*

modeling Earth's surface, 328–332

natural hazard prediction and mitigation, 466–491

natural hazards as disruptive to, 444–465

ocean-floor data analysis, 324–327

small-scale geologic changes to, 432–433, *432*

tectonic plate movement, 318–339

time scale of changes to, 433–438, *435, 436, 437, 438*

Earth system, 428

analysis of interactions within, 428–431

atmosphere, 6, 429, *429*

biosphere, 6, 225, 429, *429*

cycle of energy and matter, 202, *202*, 229, 237–240, *237, 238, 239*, 430, *430*

cycles in, 138–139

cycling of matter in organisms, 228–247

distribution of natural resources in, 6, 7, *7*

Earth surface and plate movements, 318–339

ecosystem, 400–414

energy from Earth interior, 431, *431*

geosphere, 6, 429, *429*

human impact on, 202, 203–204

hydrosphere, 6, 429, *429*

igneous rocks related to, 288–291

inputs and outputs, 138–139

metamorphic rocks related to, 296–299

natural resource availability, 360–381

natural resource distribution, 340–359

patterns of interactions between organisms, 382–399

sedimentary rocks related to, 292–295

subsystem interactions, 429–430, *429, 430, 431, 431*

time scale, 433

water on, 80

earthworm

as decomposer, 237

as food, 362, *362*

eastern gray squirrel, 551–552, *551, 552*

ecologist, 532

ecosystem, 362, 365, **528**

abiotic factors, 362

analysis of energy flow in, 402–406

biodiversity and dynamics of, 523–594

biodiversity indicating health of, 526–538

biodiversity influencing health of, 526–538, 567–569

biotic factors, 362

carbon cycle, 408, *408*

of caves, 52, *52*, 59, *59*

changes in, 546–550

of coral reefs, 526, *526*

cycling of matter in, 407–410

distribution of, 364

disturbances in, 532–533, 541, *541*, 543, *543*, 548, 561

within Earth system, 400–414

effects of change on, 549

energy pyramid, 406, *406*

energy transfer in, 402–406

eutrophication of, 548, *548*

Florida everglades, 364, *364*, 365

food chains and food webs, 403–404, *403, 404*, 406, *406*

forest, 363, *363*, 372, *372*

of forest floor, 546, *546*

habitat destruction of, 536, *536*

health of, 532, 564–569

human activity impact on, 535–538

human impacts on, 365

humans as part of, 535–538

humans' relying on, 564–567

impact of product disposal, 16, *16*

interactions in, 532, *532*, 573

keystone species in, 570–571

as level of ecosystem organization, 364, 365

levels of organization, 364–365, *365*

lionfish impact on local, 421–422, *421*

living environment, 362

living things and nonliving things in, 546–558, 561, *561*

maintaining, 562–582

natural resources from, 7, *7*, 14, *14*, 565, *565*

nitrogen cycle, 409, *409*

nonliving environment, *362*

parts of, 362–365

pond, 402, *402*

population changes in, 551–555, 561

production and distribution disrupting, 15, *15*

rain forest, 372, *372*

recovery from disturbances, 533, 550

restoration ecologist designing solutions for, 539–540

services provided by, 566, *566*, 578

society's relationship with, 16, *16*

stability of through disturbances, 532, 533, *533*

stabilization of, 544–556

water cycle, 352, 407, *407*

water distribution in, 56, *56*

wetlands, 400, *400*

ecosystem diversity, 529, *529*

ecosystem services, 7, *7*

ecotourism, 583–584

edge effect, 573

electrical energy, 120, *120*

electric conductivity of matter, 58

electromagnetic waves, 177, *177*

electron micrograph

chloroplasts, 257, *257*

mitochondrion, 259, *259*

element, 106

in chemical formula, 156

in human body, by mass, 231, *231*

properties of, 107

elephant

as consumer, 237

preservation of, *557*, 583–584

resources needed to survive, 366, *366*

Elephant Nature Park (ENP), 584

elevation

air pressure changing, 97–98, *97*

boiling point at, *98*

Explore First

Fredrich Mohs, 57
freeze, cost in U.S., 462, *462*
freeze-thaw cycle
 chemical weathering, 270
 physical weathering, 269, *269*
freezing point, 94, *94*, 95
frequency, natural hazard data,
 450–451, *450*
freshwater
 natural resource distribution,
 346–347, *346*, *347*, 352–354, *352*
 phytoplankton in ecosystem of, 249,
 249
frog, 258, *258*
fuel
 biofuel, 213–214, *213*, *214*
 as synthetic material, 211, *211*
fungal disease, 537
fungus
 as biotic factor, 372
 as decomposer, 236, 237
 decomposition by, 236, *236*
 shelf fungi, 363, *363*
 soil formation, 344, *344*

G

gallium, 85, *85*, 101, *101*
game theory, 17
Garden by the Bay, Singapore, 562,
 562
gas, 74
 changing states of, 94, *95*
 chemical reaction production of,
 144, *144*, 146, 162, *162*, 172, *172*
 convection energy transfer, 177, *177*
gas chromatography (GC), 100, *100*
gases
 attraction of particles in, 78
 kinetic energy of, 97
 as state of matter, 55, 72, 83
 in volcanos, 49, *49*
gel electrophoresis, 131
genes, increasing variety of in
 crops, 537
genetic diversity, 529, *529*
 in crops, 537

geological processes
 igneous rock, 288, *288*
 metamorphic rock, 296, *296*
 sedimentary rock, 292, *292*
geologic hazard prediction
 earthquake prediction, 475–476,
 476
 timing and magnitude, 472, *472*
 volcanic eruption prediction, 472,
 472, 473–475
geologic hazards
 described, 448, *448*, 449, *449*
 predicting, 472–476
geologic hazard, volcanic eruption
 as, 452
geologic processes
 analysis of Earth system
 interactions, 428–431
 explaining changes on Earth
 surface, 432–438
 impacts on Earth surface, 426–443
 large-scale changes to Earth
 surface, 432–433, *432*
 small-scale changes to Earth
 surface, 432–433, *432*
 time scale of Earth surface changes,
 433–438, *435*, *436*, *437*, *438*
geosphere
 Earth system, 6, 429, *429*
 igneous rock in, 290
 metamorphic rock in, 298, *298*
 rare earth elements (REE), 355–356,
 355
 sedimentary rock in, 294, *294*
geyser, 439, *439*
Gibbons, Doug, 335–336, *335*
ginseng, 536
giraffe, 233, *233*
GIS (Graphic Information System),
 485
glacier, 274, *274*, 548
glass, 6, *6*
 creating, 86, *86*
 liquid bioactive, medical, 511, *511*
 sand for, 6
 as synthetic material, 206, 210, *210*
glassworker, 86, *86*
Global Positioning System (GPS),
 474, *474*, 475

Glossopteris, 320, *320*
glove, testing disposable, 506, *506*
gluten-free foods, 308, *308*
gneiss, 296, *296*, 298, *298*
gold
 distribution of, 341, *341*, 342, *342*,
 343, *343*
 iron pyrite compared, 140, *140*
 as nonrenewable, 351, *351*
 panning for, 278–280, *279–280*
 weathering, erosion and deposition,
 278–280, *279–280*
gold particles, 62, 69, *69*
Gold Rush, 351, *351*
government, natural hazard
 mitigation, 483–484, *483*, *484*
GPS (Global Positioning System),
 474, *474*, 475
gradual changes in ecosystem, 548
graduated cylinder, 72
Grand Canyon, formation of, 285,
 285, 294, *294*, 305, *305*
granite
 as igneous rock, 290, *290*
 as natural resource, 197, 198
graph
 of bird species biodiversity, 534, *534*
 of forest coverage, *553*
 Stress-Strain Graph, 35, *35*
 of temperature, 91
Graphic Information System (GIS),
 485
graphic organizer
 for key concepts, 3, 51, 135, 227,
 317, 425, 525
 Venn diagram, *551*
graphite, 119, *119*, 197, *197*
gravel, 36, *36*
gravity
 as deposition agent, 274, *274*
 as erosion agent, 274, *274*
 tectonic plate movement, 334
 water cycle, 407, *407*
 as weathering agent, 268
gray squirrel, 551–552, *551*, *552*
Great Garbage Patch, 574
Great Lakes, glacial origin of, 274
Great Salt Lake, Utah, 523, *523*
greenhouse gas, nitrous oxide, 575

metamorphism, 296
meteor, 487
meteorite
  crater in Arizona, 427, *427*, 441, *441*
  time scale of change, 433
meteorologist
  natural hazard data, 450
  tornado data, 459, *459*
methane, *113*
  balanced chemical equation, 167
Micronesia, 570
microscopes, 108
Mid-Atlantic Ridge, 324, *325*, 434, *434*
mid-ocean ridge, 324–325, *324*, *325*, 327, *327*
mineral, **286**
  formation of, 286
  metamorphic rock formation, 296, *296*
  resource distribution, 342, *342*, 343, *343*
  within rock, 287, *287*
  rock compared to, 286–287
  rock formation, 287, *287*, 296, *296*
  small-scale geologic changes to Earth surface, 432–433, *432*
mineral resources, 565
  availability of, 6, *6*
  chemical formulas of, 158, *158*
  Mohs hardness scale for, 57
  as nonrenewable resource, 201, 350–351, *351*
  use of, *565*
minerals
  in igneous rocks, 288, *288*, 290, *290*
  natural resource distribution, 342–343, *342*, *343*, 350–351, *351*
  in sedimentary rock, 292, *292*
mining
  coal, 303–304, *303*
  impact on ecosystem, 14
  mountaintop removal, 205, *205*
  in United States, 7, *7*
Mississippi (state), Hurricane Isaac (2012), 447, *447*
Missoula Flood, 276, *276*
mitigation, **482**
  natural hazard, 482–486

mitigation plan, natural hazard, 482, 483, 485–486, *486*
mitochondrion, cellular respiration, 258–259, *258*, *259*
model
  balanced chemical equation, 167, *167*
  chemical reactions, 160, *160*, 162, *162*, 165–168, 251
  of chemical substances, 160
  of deoxyribonucleic acid (DNA), 117, *117*
  deposition, erosion and weathering, 276–277, *267*
  developing and testing, 25, *25*, 30–31, 34
  Earth's surface, 328–332
  of ecosystem changes, 526
  of elements and compounds, *111*
  of matter, 61–64
  mitigation planning, 485
  of molecules, 112–117, *112*, 125, *125*
  of objects, 63–64
  Pangaea, 330–331, *331*
  particles of solids, liquids, and gases, 76–77, *76*
  of plastic polyvinyl chloride (PVC), 115
  removal of thermal energy, 93–96
  rock cycle, 300–302
  of scale of atom, 108, *108*
  testing solutions, 25, *25*
  of thermal energy added to substance, 89–92
  types of, 34
Mohs hardness scale, 57
mole (animal), 363, *363*
molecular structure, of food, 252, *252*
molecule
  atoms bond to form, 232, *232*
  carbon as building block of living things, 251–252
  carbon-based molecules in cells, 251–252, *252*
  chemical bonds in, 232, *232*
  chemical equations and chemical reactions, 162

chemically bonded atoms, 109, 112
chemosynthesis, 243
coefficient in chemical equation, 160
compounds of, 109–110, *109*, *110*
of deoxyribonucleic acid (DNA), 117, *117*
modeling, 112–117, *112*
particles of matter, 107, *107*
structures of, 118–120
mollusk, 528, *528*
monitoring
  earthquake warning system, 335–336, *335*, *336*
  landslide warning system, 471
  natural hazard, 469, *469*
  volcano, 474–475, *474–475*
  weather/climate hazard, 478, 480, *480*
monoxide, 118
moon in Earth system, 428
Morocco, 528, *528*
moss
  chemical weathering, 270, *270*
  resources needed to survive, 366, *366*
motion, of particles, 75, 76–77, 78, 90, *90*, 95
mountain, tectonic plate boundaries and surface features, 329, *329*
mountain ranges
  matching landform data across Atlantic, 322, *322*, 323
  volcanic, parallel to deep-ocean trenches, 327, *327*
mountaintop removal mining, 205, *205*
Mount Pinatubo volcanic eruption, 453, *453*, 472, *472*
Mount St. Helens volcanic eruption, 436–437, *436–437*, 453, *453*, 483, *483*
Mount Vesuvius volcano, Italy, 457, *457*
mudslide, lahar, 454, *454*, 483, *483*
mudstone, 292
muscle, lactic acid fermentation, 261, *261*

mushroom, as decomposer, 236, 237
mutualism, as symbiotic relationship, 390

N

nail, chemical properties of, 141, *141*
National Aeronautics and Space Administration (NASA), 42, 487
National Oceanic and Atmospheric Administration (NOAA), 478, 479, *479*
National Weather Service (NWS), 478
natural disaster, 447
  climate hazards, 449, *449*
  described, 447, *447*
  geologic hazards, 448, *448*, 449, *449*, 472–475
  types of, 446, *446*, 448, *448*, 449, *449*
  weather hazards, 448, *448*, 449, *449*
  worldwide data (1995–2015), 448, *448*, 451, *451*
natural disasters
  cost of, in U.S., 461–462, *461*, *462*
  disease and, 516, *516*
natural ecosystem disturbances, 532–533
natural gas
  fossil fuel distribution, 345, *345*
  as nonrenewable resource, 201
  propane, 105, *105*
natural hazard, 446
  climate, 449, *449*
  describing risk, 446–451
  as disruptive to Earth surface, 444–465
  geologic, 448, *448*, 449, *449*, 472–475
  historical data on, 450–451, *450*
  mitigation, 482–486, *482*, *483*, *484*–485, *486*
  monitoring data on, 469, *469*, 471, 474–475, *474*–*475*, 480, *480*
  prediction, 468–471, *468*–*471*

  risk in U.S., 446, *446*
  scientific understanding, 468, *468*
  tornado data, interpreting patterns in, 458–460
  types of, 446, *446*, 448, *448*, 449, *449*
  volcanic data, interpreting patterns in, 452–457
  weather, 448, *448*, 449
natural resource, 6, 196, 340–359, 360–381
  analyzing, in creation of synthetic materials, 196–199
  availability of, 200–201, 360–381
  chemical makeup, 197, *197*
  competition for, 370–373, 392–394
  consequences of using, 203–205
  cycle of matter and energy, 202, *202*, 229, 237–240, *237*, *238*, *239*, 430, *430*
  distribution of, 6, 340–359
  ecosystem, parts of, 362–365
  evaluating the effects of using, 200–205
  factors that influence, 368–369, *368*
  fossil fuel, 344–345, *345*, 346, 350–351, *351*
  freshwater, 346–347, *346*, *347*, 352–354, *352*
  and growth, 366–369
  human impacts on, 349–354, 368–369, *368*
  life cycle of, 9–13
  limited resources, predicting effects of, 370–373
  living or nonliving, 196, 197, 202
  made from synthetic materials, 194–212
  management consequences, 203–204
  minerals, 342–343, *342*, *343*, 350–351, *351*
  nonrenewable, 16, 201, 350–351, *351*
  obtained in synthetic material life cycle, 496, *496*, 498, *498*, 501, *501*, 507, *507*

  obtaining, 9, *9*
  patterns of, 342–348
  potentially renewable, 201
  predicting effects of abundant resources, 374–376
  processing of, 10
  properties of, 197, *197*
  relationship between science, engineering and, 4–21
  renewable, 201, 202, 347, *347*
  soil, 344, *344*, 349, *349*
  sources of, 6, 196
  uses of, 6, 9–13, 21, 198–199
natural resources
  from ecosystem, 565, *565*
  properties of, 60
natural system
  changes in matter and energy, 139
  inputs and outputs, 138–139
  matter and energy in, 138–139
Nebraska, tornado data collection, 458, *458*
needs
  identifying, 26, *26*
  met by synthetic materials, 494, *495*
  resource use driven by, 8
  of society, 8, 15
negative consequences, of using natural resources, 203–204
New Jersey, flood, 466, *466*
New Zealand, tsunami warning signs, 467, *467*, 489, *489*
Nile River, 56, *56*
nitrogen-based fertilizer, 575, *575*
nitrogen cycle, 409, *409*
nitrogen dioxide, 110, *110*
nitrogen-fixing bacteria, 389
nitrogen, in human body, 231, *231*
nitrous oxide, 110, *110*, 575, *575*
NOAA (National Oceanic and Atmospheric Administration), 478, 479, *479*
nonliving things
  in ecosystem, 528, *528*, 546–558, 561
  ecosystem disturbances affecting, 532
  as matter, 54
  observing patterns in, 52–64

nitrogen cycle, 409, *409*

phototrophs, 243, 244

physical weathering, 269, *269*

producer transform sun energy into food, 236, *236*

as renewable resource, 16

sugar stored in, 252, *252*, 257

sun as energy source for, 233–234, *234*

sunlight as energy source for, 233–234, *234*, 256–257, *256*

plant material

for biomass fuel production, 211, *211*, 213

as natural resource, 197, *197*

plastic

impact on animals, 516, *516*

as synthetic material, 206, 210

plastic bag, 502, *502*, 573, *573*, 574

plastic bottle, recycling of, 23, *23*, 39, *39*, 493, *493*, 513, *513*

Plastic Bottle Village, 23, *23*, 39, *39*

plastic microbead, 574

plastic polyvinyl chloride (PVC), 115, *115*

plate tectonics, 333–334, *333–334*

platypus, as carnivore, 385, *385*

plesiosaurs, 230, *230*

pollen, *61*, 62

pollination

cross-pollination by bees, 390, *390*

as ecosystem service, 7, 566, *566*

from obtaining resources, 14

pollinator, role in ecosystem recovery, 533, *533*

pollution

reducing, 573, *573*, 576–577

from synthetic materials, 501–504

polyester, 209, *209*

polyester fabric, 493, *493*, 495, *495*, 513, *513*

polyethylene, formation of, 207, *207*, 210

polymer, 210, **210**

pond ecosystem, 402, *402*, 548, *548*

population, 365

in community, 365

competition, to control size, 394, *394*

dependent on disturbances, 556

effects of ecosystem changes on, 553–555

exponential growth pattern, 377, *377*, 378, *378*

factors influencing, 554–555

growth and natural resource availability, 367, *367*, 369, 373, *373*, 375

as level of ecosystem organization, 365

logistic growth pattern, 377, *377*, 378, *378*

predicting changes in, 551–556

size of, and feeding relationships, 388

symbiotic relationships, predicting changes, 391, *391*

Port Campbell National Park, 267, *267*, 281, *281*

positive consequences, of using natural resources, 203–204

potentially hazardous asteroid (PHA), 487–488, *487–488*

potentially renewable resource, 201

Praia do Camilo region, Portugal, 266, *266*

prairie ecosystem, 530

precipitate

chemical reaction production of, 146

copper sulfate and ammonia, 154, *154*

defined, 146

precipitation

El Niño cycles, 395–396, *395*, *396*

water cycle, 407, *407*

predator

feeding relationships, 384, *384*, 385, *385*, 388, *388*, 394, *394*

lion as, 384, *384*

role in ecosystem recovery, 533

prediction

asteroid impacts, 487–488, *487–488*

of change of state, 87–88

of climate hazards, 477–481, *477–481*

flood, 480–481, *480–481*

of geologic hazard, 472–476

hurricane, 469, *469*

of landslide, 470–471, *471*

of natural hazard, 468–471, *468–471*, 469, *469*, 474, *474*

of population changes, 551–556

of volcanic eruption, 472, *472*, 473–475, *473–475*

of weather hazard, 477–481, *477–481*

preparation, natural hazard mitigation, 483, *483*, 484

preservative, as synthetic material, 211

pressure

affecting change of state, 97–98, 103

to form diamonds, 119

metamorphic rock formation, 296, 297, *297*, 298, *298*, 301, *301*

mineral formation, 286

rock cycle, 301, *301*

rock cycle model, 301–302, *301*

rock formation, 287, *287*

sedimentary rock formation, 292, 293, *293*, 294, *294*

prey, feeding relationships, 384, 385, 388, 394, *394*

primary productivity, 253, *253*

problem, in science and engineering, 34. **See also engineering problem**

producer, 236, *236*

cellular respiration, 258

energy pyramid, 406, *406*

photosynthesis, 253

primary productivity, 253, *253*

product, 144

in balanced chemical equations, 166, 167

cellular respiration, 258, *258*

in chemical equation, 161, 251, *251*, 261

V

values, met by synthetic materials, 495, *495*

vanilla, synthetic, 212

Vanuatu islands, 332, *332*

vegetable farm, 9, *9*

VEI (Volcanic Explosivity Index), 453, *453*

Venn diagram, *551*

vermicomposting, 313–314, *313*

vinegar, 144, *144*, 163, 180, *180*, 186–187

volcanic ash
energy from Earth interior, 431, *431*
as hazard, 138, *138*, 452, 454, *454*

volcanic eruption, 452, 548–549, *549*
deep-ocean trenches, 327, *327*, 332, *332*
energy from Earth interior, 334, *334*, 431, *431*
as geologic hazard, 452
hazards associated with, 452, *452*, 454, *454*, 472, *472*
historical data, 474, *474*
Mauna Loa data, 474–475, *474*, *475*
Mount Pinatubo, 453, *453*, 472, *472*
Mount St. Helens, 436–437, 453, *453*, 483, *483*
as natural hazard, 448, *448*
prediction, 472, *472*, 473–475, *473–475*
scientific understanding, 473, *473*
sea-floor spreading, 325–326, *325*
tectonic plate boundaries and surface features, 329, *329*
tectonic plate motion, 329, *329*, 332, *332*, 333, *333*, 472, *472*
volcano monitoring, 474–475, *474–475*
Yellowstone National Park, 439–440, *439–440*

Volcanic Explosivity Index (VEI), 453, *453*

volcanic processes
eruption, 138, *138*
igneous rock formation, 288, *288*, 290, *290*

volcano
caldera, 439, *439*, 440, *440*
distribution worldwide, 472, *472*

as geologic hazard, 448, *448*, 452–457, *452–457*, 464, *464*, 472–475, *472–475*, 490
hazards, 452, 454
hot gases and liquid molten material in, 49, *49*, 454, 472, *472*
Kilauea, Hawaii, 455–456, *455*, *456*, 473, *473*
lava from, 96, *96*, 332, *332*, 452, *452*, 454, *454*
monitoring, 474–475, *474–475*
types of eruptions, 452–453, *452*
worldwide distribution, 472, *472*

volcano data, interpreting patterns in, 452–457, *452–457*, 473–475, *473–475*
building site assessment, 455–456, *455*, *456*
eruptions, 452–457, *452–457*, 473–475, *473–475*, 490
volcanic hazards, 452, 454
volcano classification, 452–453, *453*

volcano eruptions, data, 452–457, *452–457*, 473–475, *473–475*, 490

vole, as prey, 411, *411*

volume, 54
measuring, 72
patterns in, 74
as property of matter, 57, 72, 83
of solid, liquid, and gas, 73–74

volunteer, 582

W

Wallula Gap, Missoula Flood, 276, *276*

warning
tornado, 477, 479, 486
tsunami signs, 467, *467*, 484, 486, *486*, 489, *489*

warning system
earthquake, 335–336, *335*, *336*
landslide, 471

Washington, Mount St. Helens volcanic eruption, 436–437, *436–437*, 453, *453*, 483

waste
decomposition of, 237, 313–314, 344, 402
synthetic materials, 501–504, *501–504*

water
and ammonium chloride, as chemical reaction, 183, *183*, 185–186
carbon dioxide and, 251, *251*
in cellular respiration, 258–259, *258*
chemical formula for molecule of, 157, *157*
chemical separation of, 61, *61*, 106, 160, *160*
contamination, synthetic material production, 502, *502*
cycle of, 138, 202, 349, 352, 407, *407*, 430, *430*
as deposition agent, 272–275, 273–275
distribution of, 10, 56, *56*
drinking water extraction, 9, *9*, 565, *565*
on Earth, 80
electrolysis, 160, *160*
filtering solution for, 2, 47–48, *47*
gravity as agent of erosion, 274, *274*
hydrogen peroxide breakdown, 164, *164*
molecule, 110, *111*, 112, *113*, 232, *232*
monitoring quality of, 578, *578*
natural filtration of, 566, *566*
as physical weathering agent, 269, *269*
pollution of, 573, 575
producer transform sun energy into, photosynthesis, 236, *236*, 256, *256*
states of, 75
thermal energy flow from hot metal, 176, *176*
as weathering agent, 268

water energy
as renewable resource, 201, 347, 348, *348*

waterfall, 274, *274*

water molecule, 110, *111*, 112, *113*, 232, *232*

watershed-protection, 578

water vapor
condensation of, 88, *88*, 94
formation of, 89, *89*

waves, erosion and weathering, 267, 272–273, *273*, 277, 281, *281*